TESTIMONIALS

"An enjoyable and thought provoking book that provides a 'how to' guide to create and implement impactful changes as an emerging, existing and seasoned leader."
– Nicole Glasgow, Program Cordinator and Career Coach – Beaumont People

"In true Cathy Dimarchos style, this book is honest, open, helpful and inspiring. Over the years Cathy has mentored me in terms of leadership and change, and her guidance has been integral in my journey to establish and lead a successful financial services business. This book contains all the key elements, laid out in a way that makes it easy to visualise change and inspirational leadership, and create concrete steps to bring that visualisation to life."
– Belinda Smith, CEO – Eticore

"This is a unique book and couldn't be more timely. The workplace has changed dramatically in the last 18 months where all of us see the world through a very different lens. Reading this book gave me a fresh perspective on so many critical elements of leading people in today's workplace and how making some simple changes to myself and the way I communicate with others can have a huge positive impact on everyone that I work with (and live with!). For anyone that understands that people are the most important factor of any successful business this is a must read. I found this packed full of so many real life practical tips and tools and easily actionable steps that anyone can take to not just get better results from their people but to genuinely help grow yourself and the team around you"
– Jim Hall, Director SME & Accounting – Momentum Media

"I am always open to other peoples views and experiences and reading Cathy Dimarchos's book entitled Same People – different vision (great Title!) already gave me a curiosity to reading past the cover. I was not disappointed. Cathy has a warming and knowledgeable style to her writing which allows you to read and reflect at each chapter throughout the book. I found myself nodding and making notes when reading the approaches and experience Cathy has to offer. Anyone open enough to take on board Cathy's suggestions for how to Build great teams, Remove Uncertainty and in particular Finding out what your people are not telling you will bring you another level of thinking and may help your current situation or future journey."
– Linda Redfearn, Director – Evolve People

"Loved it. So much wisdom, experience, passion. It will be very well received by your readers and would be super useful for anyone in the business world – from the beginners and the experienced managers/business owners as well. This book should be the one to keep on every manager's desk, not to be shelved after the initial reading, so one can go back and revisit and refresh and reflect and follow the footprints over and over again – because we often lose focus of what's important and what matters most by being sucked into our everyday routine."

– Rita Katselnik, President – Working Solutions Agency NYC USA

"It's refreshing to see a business book like Same People, Different Vision by Cathy Dimarchos enter the market. Cathy's philosophy of investing in developing visionary new leaders today so that we can create a brighter future for us all tomorrow is the driving force behind this book. Providing a comprehensive framework for success, this book also provides practical steps to develop the skills, confidence and vision to take individuals, teams and organisations further together. Her emphasis on the power and importance of communication, emotional intelligence, relationships and connection to create change, motivate teams and achieve your goals is what sets this book apart. Same People, Different Vision is a must-read for all business leaders ready to be the change they want to see."

– Peace Mitchell, Co-founder – The Women's Business School

"Cathy has taken me on quite a journey in this book, quite aptly called 'Same People, Different Vision'. She has highlighted some very thought provoking points and has written this book in such a way, that allowed me to go through it and collect the key points that related to me and my business with ease. One of the key areas I really enjoyed in this book, was Cathy's take on how the be a conscious leader in today's world. Our world today looks so different to even just a few years ago and Cathy has highlighted the key areas we all need to review, tweak, potentially pivot and most importantly, act on. Cathy goes as far as to challenge our beliefs and encourage us as leaders in business to start with the end in mind and work backwards. This book will challenge your thinking, yet support you in your growth towards your new normal. I highly+F15:F23 recommend this book to anyone leading a team, leading themselves or just wanting to shift their perspective into a far more positive outlook in the world."

– Shar Moore, CEO / Founder & Editor-in-Chief – Femminencense

"I loved every single moment of this book. REALLY!! An authentic and brilliant insight in a world facing many different challenges. Anyone in management and leadership roles must read this book. I learnt so much and took lots of notes that have already provided an immediate benefit to my business as a CEO. Thank you, Cathy! "

– Ross Paraskevas, CEO – Instaknow Australia

"Congratulations on a wonderful inspiring debut book! Thank you for sharing your life experiences and providing an honest clear road map in all aspects of life. This book will become a classic!"

– John Paraskevas, CEO – Faraday West

CATHY DIMARCHOS

SAME PEOPLE PEOPLE DIFFERENT VISIN

developing leaders of today to
shape a better tomorrow

KMD
BOOKS

Edited by Tracey Regan
Interior design by Dylan Ingram

A catalogue record for this
work is available from the
National Library of Australia

National Library of Australia Catalogue-in-Publication data:
Same People, Different Vision/Cathy Dimarchos

ISBN: 978-0-6451669-0-3
(Paperback)

ISBN: 978-0-6451669-1-0
(eBook)

Disclaimer

The material in this publication is of the nature of general comment only, and does not represent professional advice. It is not intended to provide specific guidance for particular circumstances and it should not be relied on as the basis for any decision to take action or not take action on any matter which it covers.

Readers should obtain professional advice where appropriate, before making any such decision.

To the maximum extent permitted by law, the author and publisher disclaim all responsibility and liability to any person, arising directly or indirectly from any person taking or not taking action based on the information in this publication.

ABOUT THE AUTHOR

A multiple award-winning strategic business advisor, mentor and inspirational international speaker, Cathy is an indefatigable philanthropist who is passionate about raising the baseline of where people begin their life. Her passion is to assist people to leave a lasting imprint and create paths that enable them to lead the lives they deserve.

As a professional advisor, consultant and motivational voice, Cathy dedicates her time to a combination of people, business and situational skills, delivering tangible business toolkits and solutions to clients from every imaginable background.

Through the global financial crisis Cathy saw thousands of people destabilised, her clients facing financial hardship and unacknowledged anxiety, as well as mounting mental health issues. It was during this period she decided that she needed to do more – be more. She changed the way she approached everything, studying counselling to further understand the machinations beneath the decisions and struggles she saw day-to-day in organisational roles.

More than numerical support, Cathy goes beyond the product, or process, guiding her clients through their immediate needs, long-term options and real-time pain points.

Working across international borders, cultures and different perspectives highlighted the importance of embracing her professional lives holistically. Collaboration, acceptance and the recognition of strength in difference, became transformative – for both her, and for those she worked with. Her values took centre stage and business became honest and expressive. She believes that knowledge exchange leads to effective and sustainable outcomes.

Her time living with the Maasai in Tanzania, whilst teaching English and working in orphanages where she helped build water tanks, has led her to her mission in life – to lift the baseline of where people begin to live.

Her calling is to support others to realise their unspoken ambitions and step outside the comfort zones that regularly hold them back. Developing leaders of today to shape a better tomorrow, forms part of her philosophy, and this commitment extends to developing leaders in underprivileged and underdeveloped countries so they too may live the life they deserve.

Contents

1

RAISING THE BASELINE TOGETHER

If you had to pay for every word you use, how much less (or more) would you be saying? Would you be more conscious of the choices you make? Words make an impact on us and on those around us, yet we seem to use them a little more freely than we would if, perhaps, there were a cost associated to them.

Hi, my name is Cathy Dimarchos, and I'm *very* passionate about people. More specifically, I care deeply about the impact we have on each other, particularly through our words.

My mission is to ensure we raise the baseline of where people begin their life, and to change people's lives, dreams and aspirations across the globe. I want to help deliver the same kind of insight and passion globally, so that we can make a commitment to doing better; to *being* better as a collective.

I encourage you to join me in my commitment of giving everyone across the globe an opportunity to do things differently. Let's disrupt the current way we do business and leave a more positive footprint.

Why?

Truth be told, when you leave a footprint, others follow. And the kind of footprint you leave determines the path for others. It creates either a positive or negative ripple effect that can affect people far beyond their known circle.

When I reflect on my thoughts around the words we use every day, I see many people putting little thought into their language and the way in which they engage. Whilst we are, in general, emotive individuals, we could become more mindful and aware, so that the impact we make on ourselves and on others is a positive one.

Sadly over the years, I've witnessed many leaders, especially in moments of stress, react rather than taking a moment to reflect, seek feedback and collaborate. They have reacted and this has led to their staff being spoken to harshly or belittled. In these moments whilst looking at how to solve a situation, they have often looked to blame. I question, 'What is achieved by that?'

There isn't a clear answer, but on odd occasions, I have heard excuses – none of which warrant the action or the words. So, I have come to the conclusion it is a direct result of the footprint they have been following that has brought them to react and engage in this way.

Have you ever heard the saying, '… well they need to earn their stripes'? It's a phrase I've heard across corporations and businesses in general over the years. People often use this saying as an excuse to suggest challenges must be endured so they can understand what it's like to be a leader, or to know what others have gone through to get to a higher position.

I have a different lens, one that allows us to share experiences (both positive and negative) so that we can provide a base from where people may listen, understand and then make decisions which better serve them and those around them. Nobody needs to experience pain to know that it exists. We don't need people to endure difficult situations so we 'know the best way to do something', most certainly not in business or in life.

We want people to lift those around them, raise confidence and create a space where others feel safe, so they too can instill the same thoughts, actions and behaviours within others in their circle of impact. We can all contribute to a greater ripple effect.

I'll never forget the time I saw a gifted male senior leader, lying in the foetal position in my office. He had been continuously spoken down to and lost confidence in who he was as a human being. He could no longer manage the toxic culture and stress he faced in his working environment. This happened not once, not twice, but many times. It became a destructive pattern and his ability to contribute was diminishing with each experience.

Whilst this was reported to the board and acknowledged, their decision was not to impose changes on the CEO to improve his leadership, but for the CEO to make changes himself. There was an opportunity missed for all parties to take ownership – all leaders, the CEO and the board. If we want to see change, it must be from within ourselves. Boards, as well as CEOs and leaders, need to *show* their employees what they mean by change. They need to be the difference and this must be communicated through their actions, the choices they make, and in the words they use. No behaviours, choice of words, or actions that lead to repeated patterns where psychological safety is not maintained will deliver creativity, productivity, innovation or collaboration. If governments, corporations and businesses want to step into the ever changing world we live in and be innovative and ahead of the game, they need to consider 'what else?' and deliver a space that encourages both social and psycological safety.

I want all of us to step into our own and contribute to the changes we want to see. I want us to engage in life and work in a holistic manner.

This is not about being 'soft'. It is about being a human who wants to contribute to a better outcome for everyone.

Mahatma Gandhi famously said:

'Be the change you want to see in the world.'

This is something I strongly believe in. We have so much power to contribute to any situation and turn it around. Each of us can help transform the world by simply being more conscious with the words we use, by considering how they'll be heard, perceived and received.

So, are you with me on this journey?

If so, this book will help you see what you're capable of as a leader. It will show you how to create amazing teams who align with your vision and perform at the highest standard – people who uphold values.

But first, I'd like to explain a bit more why I care so much about this.

WHY IS THIS SO IMPORTANT TO ME?

When I was working in the bank, part of my job was to manage people's portfolios (their loans), mostly business people or clients with high net worth. It was a pleasure to be able to serve others, but was also at times stressful, since some people needed to sell their businesses or homes due to financial stress, and this on the odd occasion led to recovery action taken; yes, that meant repossession of their assets, especially during the GFC.

There was a defining moment in my career that I recall distinctly. This experience changed the trajectory of how I saw things, however, I did not realise the true impact at the time.

One night, I got a call from a client at the office. It was very late, and she was sitting in her car, in her garage, waiting with a serious ending in sight. She was anxious about the impending sale of her home; sadly her situation had led us to take recovery action and the impending sale may have led to her losing everything.

As you can appreciate, this was a stressful time for her, and a call like this so late in the evening was unusual, especially as we had already outlined the steps forward with her – one step at a time. However, this process is never easy for the client or anyone involved, and I'm so grateful she made the call that night.

It was a point of revelation for me. I talked to her for more than an hour and a half, listening to her struggles and her experiences because that was what she needed – to be heard, to be understood.

As the next few days and weeks progressed it dawned on me that despite my extensive knowledge of finance, processes, and recovery strategies, I needed to know more, to be more. There was another layer that needed to form part of what I did – it was to focus more on the people – their stories, emotions, and reality needed to form part of the dialogue. I didn't just need to ask the questions that were relevant to work, but to genuinely listen, to understand who they were and what their story was.

As individuals, we all draw from our past experiences, so my journey and lens in the process was far different from anything I could imagine for my clients. At the time, I had no similar personal experience to draw from. Over the years, I found myself in situations which led me to a path I had not originally contemplated, which would later form part of my career.

To go back to this story, the client's partner came home, ensuring she was in good hands, so the story does have a safe ending, but it was more of a positive outcome in hindsight for a different reason, as it led to a vital conclusion on my part:

I needed to do *more!* I needed to *be more!*

Because of this and a few more similar experiences, I undertook studies in a Bachelor in Counselling and Human Change. And no, I didn't just study it; I *practiced* it.

You see, there's a huge difference between reading about something – be it psychology or anything else – to that of practicing it and understanding it. This is why so many of us attend one-day events, get inspired and then, due to a number of reasons, go back to our original patterns.

You see, to truly bring about change, we need to practice, live and reflect on our new learnings; to form relationships with people, accept differences and share in their journey, to be able to better understand ourselves and those around us.

To get this kind of broadness, I spent several years doing clinical work, and later in life, I spent time in Africa; I worked in orphanages and crisis centres for babies and across cultures – I built water tanks and lived with the Maasai teaching English, learning more about their culture, and being gifted in sharing their lives. I have continued my learnings through my ongoing commitment to being among people and sharing in their lives, so that I can experience more. More recently I spent time mentoring and supporting entrepreneurs in East Africa and have been privileged that they reach out for support and guidance so I too can continue my life-learning in how I can be better and how I can do better.

These invaluable experiences have played a critical role in getting to where I am today. I know my love of learning will continue and I am by no means ready to concede that I have learnt enough, as I continue to be gifted with lessons from amazing humans who surround me daily.

Having people share their struggles in the most vulnerable of moments, as well as their vision of what they want to achieve, has allowed me to see how I can make a change. Instead of reading and learning about people, I actually go on that journey with them.

That is why raising the baseline is so important to me, and why words are so important to me.

Having an in-depth view of the way our world is today, I *know* it's time for change on a global level. And I'm confident we can do it together, one word at a time, one step at a time.

This book is a way for you to navigate your path forward and be the change you want to see in the world; standing up and guiding others with you.

Are You Ready to Join Me on This Journey?

As you join me, by reading more of this book, you are *being* more. You see, it's not me who will initiate positive changes in the world, it is you and others like you, who have picked up this book wanting to be more, to do more. No one person can do it on their own, but we can all contribute. Rather, it's the collective responsibility of each of us, and if others don't know how, this is where you can step in. Like me in my early stages of wanting to make a difference, I was not aware of *what* or *how*. I knew something did not sit right, but was lost in what that meant and what I could do.

With a different lens as you begin your new journey, think about where you were and where you are now, today, as you read this book.

I know for me, what I can do is share some of my experiences, so I can show you how you can contribute to this new world we'll create. The main goal of this book is to give you actionable guidelines that will take your leadership to an elevated level so you too can show others how.

By the time you finish this book, everything will be clearer for you, as it is now for me. You'll see what it takes to lead with influence, passion and commitment to others; to create a team that works in alignment with your values. It's this kind of unity that can truly change business as we know it today. Not only will you unlock new possibilities for you, your own business or the business you are working for, but the ripple effect of this new way of living and being will impact everyone you come into contact with.

Together, we will redefine leadership and you'll be able to tap into your full potential.

Top Takeaways

1. Words make an impact on us and on those around us, yet we seem to use them a little more freely than we would if, perhaps, there were a cost associated to them.

2. When you leave a footprint, others follow.

3. If we want to see change, it must be from within ourselves.

4. Engage in life and work in a holistic manner. This is not about being 'soft'. It is about being a human who wants to contribute to a better outcome for everyone.

5. With a different lens as you begin your new journey, think about where you were and where you are now.

II

CREATING ORGANISATIONAL ALIGNMENT

I'd like to share with you a story that perfectly highlights the importance of alignment.

Some time ago, I worked with two companies who collaborated on a project; one was an IT company and the other an organisational entity that needed a platform from them.

The IT company understood the matrix behind what they needed to do. They had a firm grasp of the coding and the technical aspect of it all, however, they weren't familiar with the organisational entity's end user.

And this is where a massive gap became obvious.

At the same time, there was a misalignment from the perspective of each business' goals and values. The IT company wanted to deliver the product as soon as possible so they could move their resources in a different direction.

On the other hand, the organisational company prioritised the utilisation of the program. Their goal was to serve their clients with a high-quality solution which was easy and functional for their clients to use.

This kind of imbalance created many significant issues. Whilst one company was focused on business outcomes, the other was focused on serving its clients; their values did not align.

Whilst I am acutely aware that in business there is a need to strive for profits, we can achieve this with a different focus, by ensuring we place people at the centre of what we do. Looking at collaborations with a 'win-win' lens and ensuring our values are aligned, will deliver best practices and an acceleration to revenue.

In this instance, the two companies didn't take the time to align values so they had a collective objective, nor did they realise they could work together to achieve a mutually beneficial goal. As a result, they failed to see the opportunity in front of them; namely, the companies could each open up a wealth of business opportunities as the end outcome could facilitate a new service that could surpass the current industry standards and deliver a new business model for both companies.

My goal here was to navigate both companies so they realised they were on the journey together, and an aligned objective would see an outstanding outcome for them both.

A proposal was tabled for the CEOs and board members of both companies to meet so we could review strategies, outlining the opportunities and the greater impact an aligned objective could deliver for both entities.

The results?

Let's look at this at a high level. Firstly, both companies now had alignment and true collaboration – instead of clashing continuously, the teams started pulling together. After many misunderstandings, they were actually happy to meet with each other. The teams were now passionate about making sure the project stayed on track.

What's more, there was buy-in from everyone involved. Everyone had a shared vision; one that motivated them to keep finding new ways of enhancing the product.

This is what happens when there's alignment. You achieve harmony, motivation, innovation and maximise devotion to the end goal. With this in mind, let's dive a bit deeper into what alignment can create.

What Happens When You're Pulling in the Same Direction?

As alignment can seem like a complex concept, you might be wondering what it is, more specifically, *what* are you aligning?

So let me explain …

Alignment is about creating a collective that moves towards the same higher goal. It's when everyone feels they're an equally valuable part of a team, on the same journey towards something bigger than themselves.

When you have alignment, you don't measure each person's contribution and compare it to others, rather, everyone plays an integral role, and the desired outcome wouldn't be possible without them. I always start with alignment in values. My values are to lift others around me and that means when one person wins, it is with the intent that the whole team wins.

The best metaphor for alignment would be in steering a boat.

Alignment happens when each member doesn't just sail on it but actually rows in the same direction, they keep an eye out for the others on the boat and make sure they stroke their stroke at the same time. This extends across any business, from the board to the CEO, the leadership teams, and every single team member; everyone's stroke and breath are perfectly in sync, so they all move the 'boat' in the right direction together.

When you have alignment, everyone knows their contribution and feels valued for it. People know their work has created the collective success which everyone enjoys.

At the same time, there's trust and appreciation between every team member. They can rely on one another to play their part, knowing it will never go unnoticed. Every effort is based on their mutual respect, belief and trust of one another.

I understand you might find this to be idealistic, some will even find it unachievable, but the reason for that is we've spent so much time believing that was the case. We have been sold the 'story' that nobody works for the collective – everyone is in it for themselves.

But trust me – it *is* possible. It *does* happen to those who are willing to go against the grain and introduce a positive change by showing others how! And for the leaders who are prepared to make this happen, who are the early adopters, they achieve astronomical results.

I want you to see there are actionable steps you can take to create this kind of alignment. Don't get sold on what others are saying or doing; be the difference, make a change – one word at a time, one step at a time. So, let's see how we can do it.

CREATING ORGANISATIONAL ALIGNMENT

The effects of creating alignment are well-researched and proven. For instance, ThinkTalent's research showed that organisations with effective communication and change programs had 3.5 times higher chances of outperforming their peers.

But at the same time, Deloitte's survey showed that only 23% of executives believe their companies are effective at aligning corporate purposes with the employees' goals.

It's time to change this statistic for the better!

But, how?

Here are some of the most effective tips for creating alignment in your organisation:

1. ALWAYS BE A PART OF COMMUNICATING THE STRATEGY

Miscommunication is one of the biggest dangers for an organisation. According to GlobeNewswire, businesses lose more than US$37 billion every year because of it.

This doesn't surprise, as effective communication is a cornerstone of alignment. How can everyone move towards the same goal unless the goal is crystal clear?

You need to be transparent and direct when it comes to communicating your strategy. You should make sure there's no room for doubt and confusion. Ensure your strategy outlines core values, purpose and vision. This allows everyone to align themselves to create the narrative around how they fit in and how they can contribute.

So, do you have a communication system that makes this happen? A framework that can spread one voice across your entire organisation? If not, this is an ideal opportunity to start creating alignment.

2. FOCUS ON THE POSITIVE (IN BOTH ACTION AND LANGUAGE)

Recent behavioural research confirmed the importance of having the right perspective. It showed that people feel depressed when they have to solve problems, but when they set a goal and reverse-engineer a plan towards it, they become full of optimism, energised, and committed.

There's a vitally important lesson to learn here:

Our perception of a situation matters so much more than the situation itself.

It's easy to highlight someone's mistakes when things are tough, but you don't want to take the easy road, you want to elevate your thinking and focus on the positives.

Why?

The way you approach a mistake won't make it disappear, but it will make a world of difference to the action others take to correct it. Belittling and shaming someone doesn't contribute to a solution. It only makes things worse. This framework drives down creativity and innovation, as well as elevating fear and repression.

But when you inspire and motivate someone to learn from a mistake, you can expect outstanding results. In fact, they will most likely not only solve the situation, but also identify an outcome that will prevent the same thing happening again.

There's always a positive angle from which you can approach a negative situation, it just might not be obvious. If you look a bit closer, you'll undoubtedly uncover the good in the bad.

So, in everything you do and say, always prioritise the positive. Once this becomes your default mechanism, you'll take a massive step towards a better outcome.

3. HELP YOUR TEAMS CONNECT THEIR WORK TO THE ORGANISATION'S VISION

This is one of the core principles of alignment. Your team members should always feel a strong relation between their work and the ultimate goal.

As soon as you make this happen, you'll give everyone a higher purpose to strive towards, and this can become an endless pool of motivation and devotion.

Consider this:

When people show up at work, they will know they'll get a chance to make a meaningful contribution. They won't just perform tasks until they're ready to go home, rather, they'll see every working day as an opportunity to get everyone closer to the vision.

Everyone wants to know their work has value and meaning. By connecting the work to the overarching vision, you'll ensure your team members feel this way at all times. People want to know they are contributing to something larger than themselves. They want to have the personal satisfaction that they are working for a company that has a greater purpose; one that wants to benefit its people, society, the community, the environment and the economy.

4. BE INCLUSIVE WHEN PLANNING

Alignment doesn't happen after you've made a plan, and yet, this is exactly how many businesses approach it. The leadership team creates a plan and then passes it on as a finished product. As a result, team members often feel you expect them to fall into line and worse still, that their thoughts and views are of no value.

On the other hand, including everyone in the planning process creates a much more inclusive appeal. Team members will see their opinions are important and valued. Instead of following a set plan, they'll have the opportunity to contribute to the creation of the journey.

Inclusive planning lets everyone put a piece of themselves into your vision. I'm sure you can see how this would make people more determined to commit themselves to fulfilling the objectives and succeeding in delivering the desired outcomes.

I'd like you to take a look at your planning process and see who you extend the invitation to; who is part of the journey? Look at ways where you can include everyone in the process. Give each team member a chance to participate, and you'll create a more holistic journey.

I realise in large corporates this may not be realistic, however, I do believe it's still achievable. It can be done in stages and each person can contribute and feed into a group discussion which is tabled to the leadership team. Nothing is impossible, you simply need to want to give each team, and each department, a voice so they feel valued and heard.

5. Reward Behaviour as well as Results

Most people who read this book will do so because they want a concrete result – and there's a high chance you're among them.

If that's the case, there's a vital mindset shift you need to make.

There's no doubt that what you'll learn in this book can help you achieve massive, tangible results, but this shouldn't be your primary focal point.

Why?

Because results are fleeting. You achieve one goal and then move onto the next. In the meantime, you wait for a reason to celebrate and reward. The issue with this is that it's a race without a finish line.

Whilst I agree that every ambitious business should keep striving towards more, it is the recognition of your people at each stage that will drive continued growth. If you only celebrate those higher results, you might miss out on an opportunity to make the journey itself more enjoyable, and worse still, give rise to an opportunity for your people to feel valued, trusted and like they are making a difference.

You shouldn't wait for an accomplishment to reward yourself or your team. Focus on rewarding good behaviour and ongoing positive practices. Praise your team for showing up every day to row the boat together and move in unity in the direction of your vision.

Why is this so important?

A better way to frame this question is, 'Why do you want to reward good results?' It's because you want more of them.

Well, perhaps consider rewarding *behaviour* for the same reason.

Much like rewarding results encourages more of them, rewarding behaviour does the same. When you encourage good behaviour, you get a team who will consistently strive towards repeating it. So rather than having specific situations worth celebrating, fill every working day with an opportunity to do so. Your workplace will instantly become brighter, and the performance of the team will undoubtedly reflect this.

6. SHOW THE DESIRED BEHAVIOUR (INSTEAD OF JUST COMMUNICATING IT)

Many executives take the word 'leader' for granted. They know they are leaders by default, more due to the fact that they manage people or run the business, but some leaders don't take an opportunity to truly *lead* their people.

I'm guessing you've heard of the concept of 'leading by example'. It relies on the premise that every leader should adopt the behaviours and patterns they want to see in others. And this is fundamental to creating organisational alignment.

Ranking higher than others doesn't make a leader. Having a 'manager' title doesn't make you a leader. It also doesn't mean your position is to tell people what you expect from them. As a leader you need to *show* people how they should act through your own actions.

Without this, there can be no alignment. The reason for that is simple, if you don't exhibit the behaviour you expect from others, you instantly create misalignment – you do one thing but expect others to do something differently.

To create cohesiveness and harmony, you must start with yourself. This is exactly why I wrote this book – for leaders. Changing your own behaviour to align with your values and match your goals, motivates others to do the same. The desired mindset and actions spill into every level of your organisation naturally.

This is a perfect example of why I continuously strive to live by Gandhi's quote. You must first *be* the change if you want to project it into the world. The moment you do this, everything will fall effortlessly into place.

As I indicated in my earlier chapter, showing others how, needs to align through your choice of words, your actions and your behaviour. It is through the whole of you, that people see how it can be done.

7. PROVIDE ALL THE NECESSARY TOOLS

This book is all about human connections and interpersonal relationships. With that said, every leader should leverage the right tools and systems to create organisational alignment.

So, do you have such tools in place? Does every team member have what they need to be their best selves?

If not, this is another area you can explore so that you can assist your team, and others around you, to raise their baseline.

You are a leader, and your people expect you to care about them. They want to know you'll support them in having the tools and skills necessary to reach their potential and move towards the ultimate vision.

For instance, your salespeople need training, education, and clear sales systems. As independent as they can be, your salespeople can't do it on their own – and they shouldn't try. The point of creating alignment is to have cohesiveness and collaboration. Everyone should be able to rely on each other to support them, regardless of their position or hierarchy.

Encourage your people to communicate their needs openly. By doing so, you'll know exactly what they believe they need to succeed and to achieve the desired outcome for the business. Give your team members everything they need to explore their full potential and enable them to succeed.

WHERE ARE YOUR PEOPLE PULLING?

I'm confident you now have a better understanding of what alignment is, and how these small measured and consistent steps will help you and your people too.

This concept alone can transform your organisation. It allows everyone to work as a collective, with a common purpose and a shared vision, and this is critical to long-term success.

When you have alignment, you focus all your resources in one direction. Instead of having talent scattered all over the place, you create a laser-sharp focus on the ultimate goal.

So, how far have you come towards making this happen? After reading what it takes to create alignment, how many boxes do you tick right now?

No matter where you are at, don't get too hung up on what may be missing. You are doing great because you have invested in yourself and the team by wanting more. These new opportunities are free to explore. And as you regularly practise the awareness of alignment, everything will start aligning naturally.

Remember that open communication is critical to organisational alignment. Being transparent and open will allow others to share their vision and their thoughts, as they strive to contribute and be part of the journey. Never make assumptions, and be sure to communicate effectively by listening to feedback while being as clear as possible. If you're not already working on alignment of values, this one change can make a world of difference to your organisation.

How so?

I'll explain in the following chapter.

Top Takeaways

1. Don't get sold on what others are saying or doing; be the difference, make a change – one word at a time, one step at a time.

2. Ensure your communication strategy outlines core values, purpose and vision. This allows everyone to align themselves to create the narrative around how they fit in and how they can contribute.

3. Be positive: Our perception of a situation matters so much more than the situation itself.

4. Give your team members everything they need to explore their full potential and enable them to succeed.

5. No matter where you are at, don't get too hung up on what may be missing.

III

WHAT YOUR PEOPLE AREN'T TELLING YOU (AND HOW YOU CAN FIND OUT)

I remember a time when I was sitting with the middle management employees of a company. I saw absolute genius in the people around me, but their time and talent were being wasted.

Why?

As I sat with them and explored their views, their values and their contributions, I heard them share what they had been 'sold' for many years from the leadership team. They had simply been asked to 'do as they were told'. As a result, they felt they had no voice and were not encouraged to speak up.

They were advised that their skill set was 'to do' not 'to think'. Worse still, there was a conflict of interest between departments and business units because there was no company alignment. A further issue arose in that there was clearly a perceived preference of key staff from the CEO, and this meant that none of the middle management could discuss their position or perspective with the CEO.

These managers did not feel valued or trusted and ultimately did not trust their leadership team or their CEO.

As you can conclude from this story, the communication in this company lacked transparency and creativity, and the culture was toxic. People weren't able to speak their truth or become their best selves. Consequently, the entire company suffered. Innovation was squashed, productivity was low, and despite some growth across the business, efficiencies were low with high levels of error.

Often when we see growth in a business, we assume we are doing well. Seldom do we take the opportunity to ask 'what else?' and 'how are things going for you, can I do anything to help you do your work better?' When we see increases in sales or profits, we assume everything is okay.

Had there been a culture that encouraged open communication, the outcome would be more positive for everyone. Team members would enjoy their work much more and reignite their passion for it. They would find efficiencies and create processes to make changes. They would collaborate and communicate with one another, and this would naturally create better results for the company.

A lack of a strong and open communication channel at any level in a business is dangerous, and it might be happening in your organisation. If people are unable to communicate freely, how can you know if there are issues which need addressing? In this chapter, I'll show you how to ensure broken communication doesn't plague your business. So, let's start with the key factor – you.

Are You as Strong a Communicator as You Think?

I don't know you, but I'd like to share something based on an abundance of experience.

It is likely there may be room for improvement. Like most of us, this is not a focal point as we consider what we need to do in our day-to-day of managing a team, or running a business.

Most of us like to think of ourselves as a strong communicator and 'people person', but in reality, this is not always how everyone, including our team, sees us.

The reason for this is that people often don't understand what we need at the end of the communication. Let me explain …

Let's say someone comes into your office to share a problem. As a leader, you're pretty much hardwired to come up with a solution on the spot. While this is a valuable trait, it comes at a cost.

It prevents us from truly *listening* to what the other person is saying.

You see, it's not possible to actively listen, and think about the solution at the same time. Our brains just aren't that good at multitasking this way. To think about how to deal with an issue, we must shift our focus from the other person to our own thoughts, and that means we're not listening as closely as we could.

So, how do we fix this issue?

You'll be glad to know it's quite simple. It takes practise, sure, but it's an easy fix.

All we have to do is to be more mindful of ourselves. When someone talks, quiet your mind and let all the information you hear come freely. If you notice your brain activating to come up with a response, shift your attention back to the other person.

With time, this will become habitual. You'll be mindful by default, and you'll start listening with undivided attention.

When this happens, you won't just hear the words someone says, you'll also be able to hear the *emotions* behind them and notice what they are NOT telling you. This is where all the secrets people don't tell you are found.

The ability to understand how someone truly feels is invaluable. It allows you to dig beneath the surface and reach the root cause of every issue. Furthermore, it makes people feel heard and understood. This is the basis of every successful relationship, business or otherwise.

As you become a better listener, you will become a better communicator. You'll be able to identify what triggers communication breakdowns.

These are very subtle triggers, which is why they go unnoticed most of the time. Mindfulness is an ideal way to uncover them. Being mindful of your own triggers, your own reactions and your behaviours, allows you to be aware of the impact you make in these moments.

Like with everything else, first we must begin with ourselves and then show others how to do it too. It is paving the way so others can follow and communication is no different to this rule.

With that said, I'd like to give you a shortcut, so that you can become a better communicator more quickly. Let me highlight some of the main subconscious reasons for poor communication.

The Triggers That Cause a Communication Breakdown

If you need proof that your communication could use some work, let me share some numbers with you.

Did know that 74% of employees feel like they're not up-to-date on company news? This was the result of a survey by Tribal Impact. The vast majority of the participants said they thought they were missing out.

Similarly, Workforce showed that 60% of companies have no long-term internal communication plan, and this makes the previous statistic all the more understandable.

But let me share a brighter number with you. According to McKinsey & Company, productivity increases by 20–25% in organisations where there's a strong connection. When people feel there is good communication and transparency within the organisation, they feel connected. This alone is reason enough to work on your communication channels, yet it's far from the only one.

To make communication more cohesive and effective, you must identify the things that prevent it. Here are some of the most common triggers of broken communication:

1. You Constantly Use Negative Language

The words you use have more power than you think, yet the majority of executives don't pay enough attention to them. They don't stop to think about the effect their words will have. Instead, they just say what's on their mind as it is.

For the longest time, people have thought of this as a purely positive trait, they've tied it with honesty and truth. But that's not really the case.

You can speak your truth in a more positive manner, and that will leave a better impact. By choosing your words *carefully*, you can be totally honest while still uplifting others. This is true in even the worst of situations. In fact, it's in the tough moments that effective communication is most important.

For instance, let's say an employee didn't get the desired result. The first instinct of most leaders would be to label this as a failure, and if this is what you communicate to the employee, you'd only make the situation worse.

The employee already knows they didn't achieve the necessary outcome, so highlighting this further with negative language will achieve nothing. The result is still the same, and you'd only make the employee feel worse than they do already.

Alternatively, you could approach this 'failure' from a more understanding and positive perspective. Instead of telling someone they failed, you could ask them what they believe went wrong. Was there anything they needed to help them achieve more? What was the lesson behind this experience which will help them do better next time? How could *you* have contributed differently to achieve the desired outcomes?

Can you see how this way of speaking is more constructive and inspiring? More importantly, you also include yourself as part of the solution process so they don't feel they are isolated or that they alone need to establish a different outcome.

If you have this approach, people won't be afraid to admit their mistakes; they won't feel the need to hide anything from you. Employees will see you're there to support them, which will motivate them to keep progressing. In fact, they are likely to also look at ways of mitigating risks and avoiding similar outcomes across different areas in the future.

2. YOU FOCUS ON WEAKNESS INSTEAD OF PROGRESSION

How do you think people get better at anything they do? Most leaders assume you can do this by working on your mistakes; if you fix them, you progress.

Except that this isn't how it really works.

If you want someone to do better, you need to focus on their pre-existing strengths.

So how does that make sense? After all, why should you work on something you're already good at?

Here's a quote from *Harvard Business Review* that summarises the answer perfectly:

> *'Although we label weaknesses 'areas of opportunity,' brain science reveals that we do not learn and grow the most in our areas of weakness. In fact, the opposite is true: we grow the most new synapses in those areas of our brain where we have the most pre-existing synapses. Our strengths, therefore, are our true areas of opportunity for growth.'*

CATHY

Let me explain this further.

If you keep focusing on someone's weaknesses, you're letting their strength sit unused. As a result, their talent gets wasted, just as I mentioned in the story at the beginning of this chapter.

Even if you work on the weakness with some results, the cost can be high. By the time you get better at something you're not good at, your existing talents may deteriorate. So now you're mediocre at something you weren't good at, and less competent in a previous area of strength.

See how it doesn't make much sense to focus on weaknesses? What you should do instead is highlight someone's talent and nurture it even further. In the meantime, find someone else who is naturally gifted in the other person's weakness. Keep nurturing everyone's unique talents, rather than trying to force a skill on someone who just doesn't have it.

The thing is, we're all brilliant at something, but there are also things we're not so good at. Progress is not about going from the negative to zero or slightly above it, it's about playing to our biggest strengths and developing them even further.

Most businesses look to match people into roles, and this contributes to declining achievements. We can deliver greater outcomes by aligning people's strengths to their roles. Think laterally, go against the grind and build a new way of looking at how to lead.

Once you adopt this approach, you'll let everyone proudly showcase their uniqueness, and this will do wonders for communication.

Gallup's survey showed that 71% of people whose employers focused on weaknesses, reported active disengagement. Conversely, 67% of those who felt employers focused on their strengths, reported high engagement. This speaks volumes about the perspective you should take.

Leading is about stepping up and being innovative; being prepared to bring about change so your people can be empowered and feel valued. How better can you deliver that, than by creating a platform which allows your people to shine?

3. You Neglect the Employee's Voice Entirely

How often do your employees speak their mind freely? If you had to rate your two-way communication on a scale from 1–10, what grade would you give it?

Sadly, the reality might disappoint you. Quantum Workplace's research shows that around half of all employees don't speak up when they want to. Yes, *half.*

This research is a perfect example of what I want to change in the business world. My mission is for everyone's voice to be heard loud and clear. I want to encourage you to make this happen in your organisation. There's a wealth of improvements that can be achieved once you do.

Take newsletters as an example. Earlier in this chapter, I reported that most employees don't feel updated on the company news, and simply having a newsletter doesn't do much on its own.

Think of this from a marketing perspective. You don't put out content for others to passively intake, rather, you do it because you want your audience to reach out and engage.

Your internal communication should work exactly the same way. Your employees need an opportunity to share their opinions freely and give feedback on what they hear.

Never underestimate the importance of employee feedback. Even if it's negative, people give it because they genuinely care. If they didn't, they'd simply give up and possibly leave.

Don't be afraid to hear what your employees have to say, regardless of whether it's positive or not. Every piece of feedback is an opportunity to introduce meaningful discussion and possible change.

Of course, when you start receiving feedback, that's when you need to focus on another thing I have discussed – active listening. If your people care enough to share their feedback, hoping to make a change, show the same care by listening carefully. Then follow up and act on the feedback you receive.

Whilst I can appreciate it may not always be possible to implement some feedback, don't let that be an excuse for you to do nothing. It is equally important to acknowledge and invite discussion so that everyone is aware it did not go unnoticed.

The connection in these situations is where the value exists – it is in these moments that people feel they are valued enough to be heard. With time, you'll create a more open stream of productive and honest communication.

4. You Don't Hold Regular One-to-Ones

There's no one perfect way to communicate with everyone. Each of your employees are different, and you must keep these differences in mind.

Some people are confident about speaking in large groups, while others lack this sort of confidence and keep quiet unless you're in a more private setting.

Because of this, you can never go wrong with one-to-one meetings. Those who can speak in groups can do so in private as well, and those who can't will relax and open up to a discussion.

Plus, one-to-one meetings allow you to learn more about each person in your organisation. You can discover their communication style and adapt to it. This is a topic of its own, so I'll cover it in more detail later.

For now, all you need to know is that one-to-one meetings offer a variety of benefits. They build stronger relationships and make people feel valued as you'll set aside a timeslot just for them.

As for the structure, your one-to-one meeting can look any way you want. It can be an informal chat about what's going on in the workplace. You can discuss ideas, progress and other important matters in a laid-back setting.

Alternatively, you can hold formal and scheduled meetings which follow a certain structure. This way, everyone will know exactly what you'll talk about, and they'll have enough time to think about it.

Be mindful that whilst you are leading these discussions, they are not about you, so ideally allow your staff to guide in how they best benefit from these discussions.

So how do you choose the right meeting type?

5. You Need to Understand Each Person's Preferred Communication Style

As mentioned, every team member has their own communication style. Some people may get nervous when they have to talk in person, they might prefer emails or other forms of written discussion.

Similarly, some employees want to keep every conversation strictly professional, while others appreciate you asking them how things are going in general.

In my experience, many leaders don't take enough time to understand their employees' preferred communication style, yet this is critical to ensuring that no secrets are kept from you.

No-one should understand the employees better than the person leading them. When you know how your people communicate, you can set up a system which allows everyone to speak their truth, and they'll be fully comfortable with doing so.

Bring a few random people from your organisation to mind; do you know how they'd like you to approach meetings and other communication channels?

If the answer is 'no', or you haven't thought about it, there's another opportunity for you to improve a critical aspect of your organisation. Get to know your people, approach them in a way they're comfortable with, and they'll open up without holding back.

If this is something you are doing for the first time, be mindful that people may want to make a change, so always check in with them to see if what you're doing is still working – never assume that because they previously suggested one thing, that is where they want to stay.

BECOME A POWERFUL COMMUNICATOR

Is there anything you might want to change between what we have discussed here and your current communication prowess? If so, be prepared to give things a go. Do it your way and be open to trying things differently if it doesn't work out for you first time around.

Often leaders are not aware that their communication could use some work. Don't worry, we have all been there and we all continue to learn and adapt. The key is to keep striving for improvement so we don't become stagnant. If at any stage we feel there's no way forward, the best we can expect is to stay in the same place.

Allow yourself to explore your communication style with honesty. See what you can do to get everyone in your organisation to speak freely and without reservation. No matter how good we currently are, we can always be better.

Remember, it all comes down to the choices we make with our words. Every message you release into the world has a profound impact on those who hear it. You get to choose if that impact is positive or negative.

How?

By simply asking yourself how your words will be received. Is there a chance that the message you deliver may hurt someone? Could you reframe your sentences in a way that empower rather than denigrate?

I have absolutely no doubt that you can!

Like every other skill, communication gets better with practice. With time, positive frames will start to come naturally, and I guarantee you'll see the impact of your efforts. In fact, you will not only see it in what you do, but you will notice the changes in your team and the way in which they too choose to communicate.

Whilst communication is an integral part of alignment, it's not the only one. In my next chapter, I'll discuss another cornerstone of cohesiveness and harmony.

Top Takeaways

1. A lack of a strong and open communication channel at any level in a business is dangerous, and it might be happening in your organisation.

2. As a leader, you're pretty much hardwired to come up with a solution on the spot. While this is a valuable trait, it comes at a cost.

3. To make communication more cohesive and effective, you must identify the things that prevent it.

4. Leading is about stepping up and being innovative; being prepared to bring about change so your people can be empowered and feel valued.

5. Don't be afraid to hear what your employees have to say, regardless of whether it's positive or not.

6. Allow yourself to explore your communication style with honesty. No matter how good we currently are, we can always be better.

IV

INCONSISTENCY CREATES UNCERTAINTY (WHICH DESTROYS TEAMS)

I'm highly conscious of my footprint and while I may not always get it right, it is one thing I continuously look back on to make adjustments as I strive forward. My footprint does not only relate to work, but across all areas of my life, as it's one of my core values. No matter what I do, I seek out this type of consistency.

I have two businesses, and the values in one are aligned with the values in the other, and likewise, both are aligned with my personal values. I learned how to make my own detergents, soaps and various other natural products because of this footprint mindfulness, and because I believe buying organic or natural products should not only be available to those who can afford it, but to the mainstream of the population. I believe these products can be sold at a reasonable and affordable price despite current retail price points. I stand by my values and these beliefs in every-thing I do – in my personal life and in my business life. It is also the reason why I say, 'Bring the whole of you to work.' When I made the transition that I shared in my story to 'do more' and 'be more', it wasn't just a business decision. I didn't simply go straight from being a banker to what I do now.

Rather, I made a lifelong commitment.

My values will not be compromised! In my actions, relationships, engagements and in the messages I share, I *will* speak my truth. If I'm to pay attention to my footprint, I must do so consistently across everything I do.

So why does this matter to me so much? What makes consistency such a powerful concept?

You see, consistency and the truth to your whole self are contagious. It inspires others to live their lives in the same fashion. It creates less stress while skyrocketing creativity and freedom.

Consistency creates order, and provides clarity and wholeness. It connects people and their actions, thereby contributing greatly to alignment.

People know where they stand, they know where you stand and don't have to second-guess themselves or the situation. They feel safe and believe they are part of the bigger picture because they know what's going on.

On the other hand, inconsistency has the power to stagnate people. It creates a state of uncertainty and elicits fear, and that makes it impossible to develop trust. It's this uncertainty which prevents teams from aligning with their leaders.

So, how do you avoid this? How do you stay true to yourself, effortlessly, at all times? These are some of the questions I'll answer in the next chapter. Lets dive a little deeper into the relationship between consistency and alignment.

AVOID UNCERTAINTY AND FEAR

Entrepreneurs are usually strong visionaries. They have incredible ideas and are able to see a bigger picture. Executives position themselves so that they can bring the right people together; they get everyone excited and passionate about the idea and work on strategies which support their people in laying out the milestones so they can move forward.

As they work together to roll out a new project, everyone is aligned and knows their place – they know how they will be contributing and feel part of the team.

But then, seemingly out of the blue, there is another idea. And since resources are not unlimited, they look to their people seeking more from them, or they move them onto the new project.

In these instances, all those positive feelings about the previous project vanish with it. The initial idea is set aside, and people have to immediately transition into the next one, or take on a double load.

How do you think this makes people feel? I've seen it many times, and I can tell you it's not a positive experience.

This inconsistency creates insecurity and fear. It makes people think they no longer know where they belong, and more so, that they have no clarity of the way forward. They were part of the old vision and now everything is different. Naturally, teams struggle to understand where they belong.

You can see whilst any new project is exciting, as it indicates growth, the key remains in the communication. No matter how large or how small a project is, clarity and continuity is needed. The alternative of chopping and changing or overloading staff, brings about chaos at all levels.

Having a vision of the way forward is important and needs to be shared so everyone feels they belong, and they know how they will be contributing. However, it is equally important to be consistent and keep the communication lines open.

When we chop and change, be it for the ultimate goal or just the day-to-day communication, it disrupts the previously created alignment. There's no order anymore, just confusion, disappointment, and even fear.

In saying this, consider the alternative. Let's say there are no major shifts in ideas. A plan gets developed, and everyone follows it through to its completion.

This results in an uninterrupted flow, ensured by consistency. Everyone knows their role, and they can be certain it won't change for any reason, other than enhancements. Team members have the safety that allows them to aim high and do their best work. This is what I refer to as 'psychological safety' and it is in this space that people perform at their best.

In one style, you get to create a firm structure that everyone can rely on. People *crave* structure because it makes things easier and smoother for them. They know what they need to do, and they know how they are contributing to the bigger picture. Whereas, the opposite brings about confusion, lack of productivity, and fear

Every organisation, no matter its type, needs some type of structure. When you have it, everyone knows their contribution, and they'll do their best to offer it.

But wait … where does change fit in? I hear you say. *After all, isn't this whole book about impactful changes?*

Yes, and while consistency and change seem like polar opposites, this actually isn't true. Positive, meaningful change *needs* consistency as its foundation.

How so?

When there's consistency, change can happen smoothly and naturally. It doesn't get forced by the leader onto the team. Rather, everyone takes part in it, because they're a cohesive whole. Change isn't a sudden occurrence, but a collective decision and effort. From this perspective, impactful change can be initiated effectively.

Furthermore, when change is anticipated and forms part of the accepted culture, it is embraced as opposed to feared. Change, in reality, is part of our daily life, so if we accept that something will inevitably change, although we may not know when or what, we create a different mindset around it.

What Happens When You Get This Right?

So, I explained what consistency does in theory. Now, I want to show you how this looks in practice. Microsoft is a perfect example of what you can achieve with consistency and alignment.

We all know this company as a titan of the tech industry, but from the inside, nothing looked this bright for a very long time.

Even though Windows and Office became ubiquitous, Microsoft struggled to hold its share of the market.

Why?

From my perspective, looking in, it appeared that its teams kept moving in scattered directions. Leadership seemed to jump from one product to another, trying to cover as much ground as possible. And this resulted, in my opinion, in many watered-down efforts that didn't amount to much.

It wasn't until 2014 that things changed from the ground up. Well, technically from the top down, as Satya Nadella stepped in as the new CEO.

Seeing the internal wars that were plaguing the company, Nadella initiated a major restructuring initiative. Up until then, I believe Microsoft's teams would have felt more like competitors than a united whole working towards the same vision.

To turn this around, Nadella introduced a new mission statement:

'To empower every person and every organisation on the planet to achieve more.'

And this vision started happening from within, as Nadella began by empowering his own people first.

This happened in many ways. The most meaningful change was that platforms and products were no longer separate groups. Each employee began focusing on a smaller group of goals that they all shared.

These new goals included:

- More personal computing
- An intelligent cloud platform
- Reinventing business processes and productivity

And after years of what seemed like a constant tug of war, there was finally alignment, created largely by consistency. Everyone knew exactly what the new mission was and got on board with it. More importantly, the company stayed true to its mission.

The result?

All you need to do is look at Microsoft's stock price. At the beginning of 2013, the stock price was US$26.74. As of July 2020, it's US $210.70!

This is the kind of result you can achieve with consistency. In just over seven years, Microsoft increased its share price by over 800%.

So, if you needed proof of how valuable consistency is, you now undoubtedly have it. Let's see how you can create it.

THE MISTAKES YOU HAVE TO AVOID

As we have seen earlier, consistency is a necessary prerequisite to change. In the change management process, you may make mistakes that lead to inconsistency.

To ensure this doesn't happen, here are the most common traps to be on the lookout for:

1. FAILING TO ESTABLISH A COMPELLING CASE FOR THE CHANGE

Your motivation behind a change may be different from your employees', and this misalignment can be risky.

You need buy-in from everyone in your organisation to initiate change properly. To ensure you get it, you must communicate a clear and powerful reason behind the change, so that you get everyone to pull in the right direction. The message you deliver needs to be inclusive and give clarity. This stage requires a great deal of consideration in the words you choose to use.

Why?

Because failing to deliver a message that ignites, empowers and includes everyone involved, will leave people feeling as if they don't matter. They will feel like you're forcing a change, as opposed to seeking their approval to join you. This is especially true for those on the frontline and at lower organisational levels, as they may not be able to share your perspective by default. Being able to explain clearly why the change will benefit everyone is integral. This way, you can create the kind of unity that's vital for successful change.

2. NOT HAVING A DETAILED STRATEGY IN PLACE

Related to the above, another thing you must communicate clearly is the change strategy. After all, it's the roadmap to the outcome you want to create.

Everyone will have a role to play in the strategy. What your team members used to do may not be the same as what is needed in the new role. Without a straightforward, detailed explanation, you'll create confusion and will lose unity.

To prevent this, it's important that you bring the right people together so you can formulate a clear process map with all the small measured steps needed to move forward.

Once you've outlined the strategy, make sure every team member has access to it, regardless of their position. Consistency is largely about ensuring that everyone is on the same page, and this transparent approach makes it happen.

Encourage your people to ask questions about the strategy. Let them provide feedback, particularly related to their role. Bring all areas of the business together to review the strategy and ensure all the interdependencies flow into one another and achieve the outcomes desired as a holistic project. This way, you can ensure that everyone understands their part and the impact they have on any other part of the business.

3. OVERSIMPLIFYING THE SCALE OF THE CHANGE

Before you initiate any change, you must know precisely how it will impact every part of the business, each department, and the various systems involved. Sadly, many leaders don't have the ability to see this level of detail. Rather, they focus on the impact on the company's overall performance and a few key factors (I should point out that this is fine, but it also highlights the need to include the right people at each stage).

Oversimplifying can be very dangerous. It leads to you not understanding the full impact the change will have, and some parts of the business might suffer as a result. The same goes for your people; oversimplifying can lead to not taking the time to see if the change is positive for everyone.

A natural result of this is likely to be resistance from your team members. If you don't consider the impact the change will have on them, and they do resist, you may have to make many more changes than those in your initial strategy.

So my advice is, don't rush the planning process. Leave enough time to see how every part of your business will react to the proposed ideas. Finalise the strategy only when you're confident you've left no stone unturned. I have often asked the question, 'What would you rather have, an ending you didn't want or a starting place you had not considered?'

4. Being Inconsistent in Your Involvement in the Change

Many people suffer from an initial burst of motivation that seems to disappear over time. You might be excited about an idea when it first comes to you, but as you go about executing it, you notice yourself cooling down. Consequently, you start being less and less involved in the change.

While this is a common occurrence, you must do everything in your power to avoid it. Persistence is critical in change management, so there's no room for a severe drop in motivation.

The moment you start feeling demotivated, your employees will notice it. They'll see you don't care about the change as much as you used to, so they'll stop caring as well. This is how the vast majority of changes fail to execute successfully.

This also ties into my earlier suggestion of 'showing', not 'telling'. This is a perfect situation where the importance of *doing* what you want others to do will shine. After all, you can't expect your people to remain excited and motivated about your idea if you don't continue to show the same excitement as before. Always showcase your determination, even on days when you don't feel motivated. This form of consistency will keep everyone's eyes on the prize and deliver the desired results.

5. Changing Your Mind Halfway Through

This is possibly the mistake with the most detrimental results. Few things can cause disruption as much as changing your direction out of nowhere, and there are many reasons for this.

First of all, the resources you initially used to create the change will go to waste. As change is a process rather than a single action, it takes time to see the desired results. Pulling the plug too soon is a sure-fire way to waste money, time and other resources.

What's even more damaging is that you'll lose your people's trust. Imagine if someone got you excited about something new, only to say it wasn't a good idea halfway through the execution. You'd feel foolish that you believed in the idea in the first place. That's exactly how your team feel if you give up on a new strategy without seeing it through. They may even think, 'What wasn't I told? Did they know this might fall over but still ask me to work on this?' So, how do you prevent yourself from 'changing your mind'?

Well, you need to be proactive. You must gain confidence to follow through to the end of the planning process. Don't begin executing a change strategy if there's any room for doubt. Plan carefully, involve your team in the process, and don't stop until you reach the end goal.

Importantly though, while I am suggesting you keep going with your proposed strategy, you must also still consider that there will likely be pivots and changes along the way that enhance the end result. Working with your team and reassessing each stage after their feedback, will keep everyone inclusive and focused on the desired outcome.

CONSISTENCY IS KEY

Consistency and alignment always go hand in hand. As you saw in Microsoft's example, being consistent across everything your organisation does, is vital to growth. It stops your people from competing and allows them to truly collaborate.

Make no mistake – there are many stories similar to Microsoft's. Companies who manage to ensure consistency can achieve outstanding results. This makes sense as people are, without a doubt, the most important resource in any organisation. If they can't work together towards the same goal, nothing else will compensate to achieve the desired results.

Besides, consistency is important on both personal and professional levels. I shared with you earlier the importance of involving your whole self, and this ties in with being consistent with everything you do. If you can make this happen, your organisation can reach astronomical heights.

Of course, you can't do it on your own. The point of this book is to help you create alignment with everyone in your organisation.

To do this, you must first build a high-performing team.

This is easily one of the biggest concerns for leaders, especially now as businesses, corporates and even governments find themselves in an ever-changing landscape. How do you find employees who will grow with you and help turn your vision into a reality? How do you elevate your managers to lead in a way that will have their people wanting to strive for higher outcomes?

The following chapter will discuss this in great detail.

Top Takeaways

1. Consistency and being true to your whole self are contagious. It inspires others to live their lives in the same fashion.

2. Having a vision of the way forward is important and needs to be shared so everyone feels they belong, and they know how they will be contributing.

3. Microsoft is a perfect example of what you can achieve with consistency and alignment.

4. Communicate a clear and powerful reason behind the change, so that you can get everyone to pull in the right direction.

5. The moment you start feeling demotivated, your employees will notice it.

6. Consistency and alignment always go hand in hand. It stops your people from competing and allows them to truly collaborate.

V

How to Build a Team

Leaving my job to start the next phase of my life, was undoubtedly one of the most challenging things I've ever done. It's not that I was afraid for myself and what the future held. In fact, I was excited to open this new chapter to see 'what else?' The reason it was so hard for me to leave, was the relationship I had with the people I worked with. You see, my work colleagues, my team weren't only committed to the business or their work; they were also committed to *me* personally, so I felt an obligation to make sure they felt safe and secure as I stepped away

Why?

This answer has taken me some time to reflect and take on board. The underlying answer is that as we grew as a business, we grew as a collective, and I showed them I truly cared about them; I cared genuinely and deeply.

It was important to me that I not only knew them as individuals, but I had an understanding of their family and the things that mattered to them. I knew not only the birthdays of each of my team members, but their children's. I was always genuinely keen to hear how their weekend was on a Monday morning, and on special occasions I'd write handwritten notes which showed how much they mattered to me.

Whenever one of my employees was sick, I'd send them home to ensure they had a speedy recovery. I'd check in on them regularly, not because I wanted them back to work as quickly as possible, but so they knew I was thinking of them and that their health came first. Likewise, if anyone in their family was sick, and they came into work, I would be there to support them. I'd tell them to go home to be with their family.

People do matter – they are the most valuable asset in every business – no matter what.

Whenever we onboarded a new project, the team rallied to support one another, myself included. I listened carefully to what every person had to say and how the project would impact them. I didn't just do this from a business perspective, I wanted to get to know my team on a personal level and see how each change would make a difference in their lives. This gave me an opportunity to get to know how my staff thought and enabled me to review and reflect on their strengths, so that as the business grew, I had a better understanding of what they liked, how they behaved and where their strengths lay.

I want to share here that everyone considered me a tough leader. My team would openly say, 'Cathy, you are tough but you are fair …' and I took that on board. It was important for me to know and understand what it meant for them too.

For me, being fair included being mindful and this is something I consistently strive towards today. Building genuine relationships with every member of my team is important. When you can achieve this, people are open to challenges, and change. To be honest, I didn't always get it right and I still don't, but I am in pursuit of it. It is through these values that I have been able to gain trust and build meaningful relationships. When I consider the feedback on being 'tough', I recognise that I stretch my team and always ask them to consider 'what else?' I encourage them to make changes as required, as they are at the coalface and know what works and what doesn't. It is the way I have worked to lift people so they are performing at a higher level – one they have often thought was beyond them.

So, when I was ready to move on, it was challenging for all of us. For many, there was a strong desire to follow me, and as a result, this was terrifying for me. I didn't want my departure to bring about disruption. I loved the business and what we had achieved.

I cried for the next two months as we worked together to keep the team focused on the future and the opportunities that would come about from the new path forward. I wanted to ensure their belief in themselves and the new leadership would remain strong, and that they would continue to develop and be aligned.

At the time, I had two main goals.

The first was to make sure my team felt safe, and stayed loyal and committed to one another. I wanted them to feel secure and to keep their existing jobs that gave them security.

My second goal applied to the business as a whole. I wanted it to remain stable and keep surging forward. It was a part of me, part of us all, and it was important to me that they kept steering forward.

I'll always remember the unique bond I shared with my team. Everyone felt valued, supported, and respected. There was no room for negative behaviours and patterns, and whilst there may have been differences, those differences were valued. With such a team by your side, there's no limit to what you can achieve. I will always be grateful to each of them for their commitment and loyalty, as they too helped me to grow and develop along the way. And of course, I want you to be able to create such a team.

Whilst building such a team may at times be a long process, it is most definitely worth it. It's important to remember that, as humans, we are all complex, which directly impacts our interpersonal relationships. This is why I have devoted this chapter to helping you see what it takes to build a high-performance team.

CREATING YOUR HIGH-PERFORMANCE TEAM – THE 6 TIPS

Building a team devoted to high performance takes a lot of work, but it's more than worth the effort. Once your team is a cohesive whole, achieving every new goal becomes effortless and enjoyable.

If you're not sure how to start creating such a team, here's some strategies you may find helpful:

1. LEARN ABOUT YOUR PEOPLE

Every person is unique – no doubt about that. Honour this uniqueness and account for it when creating your team.

The way I see it, many leaders don't get the order of things right when hiring. They outline what they need first, and then look for a person who ticks the right boxes. They look for skills, and by doing so, leaders fail to address the important aspects of their employee's personality.

Of course, you should always look for people who share your organisation's core values, but take some time to truly understand what makes someone tick. Learn about your employees' dreams, motivations and priorities. You'll find many people who fit your desired profile on the surface, but really you need to dig much deeper. For instance, being a team player is somewhat of a cliché. Everyone puts it on their resume because they know it's what an organisation will look for, however you must know why someone wants to work in a team and what they expect from teammates. How do they see themselves contributing as part of a team? Some people will care about unity and emotionally supporting a team, others will want to keep things more practical and rational. It will prove invaluable if you take your time to understand the core values of everyone on your team.

I've already shared the results of doing this in my story at the beginning of this chapter. I took the opportunity to get to know my team, which allowed me to form meaningful relationships.

And that's the reason why we connected so well. I wasn't just their co-worker, or their manager – I was a friend, supporter and a true leader who genuinely cared. Position yourself this way by learning about your people, and you'll quickly see how connected everyone can be.

2. ELEVATE PERFORMANCE (INSTEAD OF EVALUATING IT)

Many leaders believe performance evaluation is critical to success. It allows you to see how far you've come and what it takes to move forward.

While this is true to some extent, however, if not done with the right intent it can also create segregation. I find the way some companies structure their evaluations could use some work. More specifically, they need to focus on elevating and uplifting, instead of evaluating; they need to look at performance as a team.

Many managers see performance evaluations as a tedious routine task for each of the staff individually. As such, they try to get it over with as quickly as possible and 'get back to work'. If this is your approach, perhaps there's a mindset shift you could consider.

Look at performance evaluations as an opportunity, not a task. Because that's what it truly is – an opportunity to check in with your people and support them as individuals and as a team. Don't just go over the statistics and numbers, use it as an opportunity to ask them how they feel about their work. I can hear you say, *Feel? – that's soft,* but if you don't know how your employees feel about what they are doing, you will not be able to understand how to uplift them and encourage them to strive for excellence in their position.

This is an opportunity to see if there's something they need either as a team, or as individuals, to increase their performance and overall satisfaction. Make no mistake – there will always be something. You just need to ask and allow them to feel 'heard'. Ask if there is something you, as their leader, could have done differently to secure a better outcome for them in their goals. You see, these evaluations are also a great way for you to reflect on yourself. Be prepared to listen so you understand what changes you too can bring about.

Another suggestion is to consider bringing teams together so the evaluations are done as a collective. It is important to recognise that no one individual can achieve success on their own. We are all reliant on each another to do our part, so that we can successfully reach the end goal.

Bringing everyone together and encouraging communication to take place, will enable people to share their experiences and gain insight on the various interdependencies that exist within the business. This practice evokes unity, trust and transparency.

So, take every evaluation as a chance to strengthen and empower your employees and your teams. Celebrate their achievements as individuals and as a team, and show them how valued their work has been. Focus on the positives and work collaboratively in identifying specifics to work on, in order to deliver successful outcomes as a team moving forward.

3. BE INCLUSIVE IN ALL THAT YOU DO

Feeling like you don't belong in a team is one of the heaviest negative emotions. It leads to isolation, demotivation, and ultimately, poor performance. Employees who feel this way are almost certain to give up at some point.

For this reason, try being more mindful and focus on inclusion, if you want to have a high-performing team. Everyone should feel equally valued and supported.

So, what are some concrete ways to ensure inclusivity?

First of all, make sure everyone within the team has access to the same information. This ties into my earlier comments on communication channels, just because someone performs better doesn't mean they become a priority or the centre point of communication. Everyone should have an equal opportunity to grow on both personal and professional levels.

In addition, always spread your projects fairly across team members. There's a tendency many leaders have to give the toughest projects to the best-performing members. At first glance, this seems like a logical idea, as you can rely on a particular employee to do a good job, but it's exactly this kind of prioritisation that can drive a wedge between people.

When someone sees they're not getting a chance to prove themselves, they are very likely to stop trying. They will start to believe you don't trust them enough with the more responsible and meaningful tasks.

With this in mind, consider aiming towards being 100% inclusive with everything you do. Make people feel they are truly a part of a supportive and equal collective. You can always reward those who get better results, but don't exclude those who are not there yet. Give people a chance to prove themselves, and they'll positively surprise you. And be there for them if they need extra assistance or advice to get the task done well.

4. HELP TEAM MEMBERS CONNECT WITH EACH OTHER

Just because you're a leader, it doesn't mean you have to 'hold the hands' of your employees. In fact, you should do the opposite. Your goal should be to create a self-sustaining team who can drive results without your direct involvement at all times.

Just like employees need to have a strong relationship with you, they should have it with each other. Every team member should be able to rely on their colleagues to motivate and support them.

In this manner, your job isn't to gather people together and give them instructions, but to foster meaningful connections which will fuel a high-performing team.

But, how?

The good news is there's no shortage of ways to make it happen.

Firstly, you can pair people up and have them work together for some time (I call this 'shadowing'). This will give them one-on-one time to get to know each other better. Then, you can switch up the pair and nurture this closeness across your whole team.

Allowing a strong performer to have someone shadow them, is not about having someone to delegate to, but more about enabling the lesser experienced person to learn and understand what differences can be made to deliver better outcomes.

The key in this relationship is to model behavior so that it can be learnt and passed on. It is not just doing, but showing and explaining why you take one action over another. Imagine the impact if you took a different course, allowing open discussion so the person with less experience can also contribute to the decision-making along the way.

In addition, you can have regular team building sessions full of exciting and constructive exercises. The options are endless when it comes to team building ideas, so find the activities your team wants to engage in.

Finally, don't keep it strictly professional. Host get-togethers outside of the workplace every once in a while. This gives people an opportunity to bond outside of the office, and a change of scenery will likely help them relax and open up.

It takes time to build strong relationships between team members, but the harmony and alignment you'll achieve when relationships are formed, is well worth the effort.

5. RECOGNISE CONTRIBUTIONS

When you assign tasks, you have a good idea of why you're giving specific things to each person. You know your people's unique strengths, so you want to match them with corresponding tasks.

But are you communicating these reasons to your team members? If not, you can (and should) look to introduce this as part of your communication strategy as soon as possible, as this will see you get an instant increase in morale and performance.

Telling employees why you've assigned a certain task to them comes with many benefits. First of all, they'll see that you know them and think about their skill set. Employees will recognise your effort to understand them, and they'll undoubtedly appreciate it.

Your team members will also feel proud of their unique strengths. They'll want to nurture them further because they'll see a reward for doing so. When a person sees that you're confident in their skill to assign them a specific task, they'll want to hone that skill even further.

This can also be an opportunity to bring in the 'shadowing' I mentioned earlier. Matching an experienced person with someone who wants to enhance their skills in a similar area is a great way to build teams and create alignment.

Don't forget to consider and share any feedback coming from colleagues, partners and, of course, clients. Your employees will appreciate that others have recognised their commitment and found their work valuable. Sharing this with the whole team encourages other team members to look at opportunities, and more importantly, to celebrate the wins of their peers and colleagues. If any received feedback isn't positive, find ways to make your staff feel supported. Ensure that nobody feels as if they've failed. Instead, highlight the wins and ask them how you can help support them to achieve better outcomes in the future.

6. Offer Development Opportunities

The vast majority of people want to know they can grow and progress within a company. More specifically, research has revealed that 87% of millennials find this important.

And yet, I have seen many people go to work, only to perform their tasks until the clock says it's time to go home. Whilst you might look at this as a 'norm', I can share that it need not be. If we want to encourage higher engagement levels, then we need to find ways to inspire our people and motivate them. It is important our staff consider that their work is 'more than just a job'.

Let's create an atmosphere of motivation and commitment. Staff in general, especially millennials, are not motivated by salary alone; they want to know they are contributing to a bigger picture and to a greater cause. They also want to know they will have opportunities to grow and develop, personally and professionally. It's important we look at aligning their goals with their personal objectives and achievements. By identifying where in the business this can work for them, this can also work for you, as their leader. This is why communication and open discussion brings about transformation and change whilst aligning everyone.

Showing your team they can be better in many aspects of their lives, creates a psychological safe space, where they know they can speak freely, be creative and learn at the same time. Let them see that you care about their personal and professional development. If you can help people achieve their most important goals, they'll do the same for you.

Teams That Bond, Perform!

It's extremely hard to achieve your goals if your team doesn't work as one. If it's 'everyone for themselves', you'll see several issues arise, you won't have alignment, and this will make for a difficult environment for everyone to work in.

Some employees will see their colleagues as competitors, and unlike what many people think, this won't drive better results. It's not the kind of 'healthy competition' which motivates people to get better. In many cases, this behaviour only creates a toxic atmosphere where people undermine each other to show themselves as superior.

A more considered approach, is to focus on collaboration and support. Release the pressure by showing people they don't have to fight for progress or position. Instead, show them they are free to express themselves fully, knowing they have each other's back.

If you create such an environment, you'll remove many destructive patterns and behaviours. Your people will show up every day knowing they'll get a chance to contribute as one, and will deliver their best work. Plus, they'll be happy to see their teammates and spend time with them.

The average person spends a huge part of their life at work. As a leader, it's your responsibility to ensure they see fulfilment and meaning in their work. After all, that is what most people want from their workplace; to know they are contributing to something bigger than themselves. I will make some recommendations on this, in the following section.

The next chapter demonstrates how you can introduce these changes successfully.

Top Takeaways

1. Knowing your people so that they feel like they matter is the key to having a happy and thriving team.

2. Reward behaviour as well as performance especially when people are elevating each other.

3. Ensure your message is communicated across all areas of the business so that everyone feels included.

4. Contribute to your teams personal development as well as professional development. It is importation to provide opportunities for them to follow a path that will make them happy rather than what you want.

VI

BE THE CHANGE YOU WANT TO
SEE (AND OVERCOME CHANGE RESISTANCE AS YOU DO)

Here's something to consider.

As an individual, you have the power and ability to bring about *so much* positive change to the world. Every one of us has the capacity to tap into their full potential and create a positive impact, but we often think that as one person, little can be done.

For this reason alone, I ask you to take an opportunity and be one of the first to embrace change.

I earlier shared Gandhi's message that you must be the change that you want to see in the world, and to this day I continue to work at upholding that message with everything I do, no matter how big or small.

This is especially true in my relationships. Whenever I meet someone, I first take the time to listen so I can understand what they would like me to hear. I look for other things that they are telling me – through their non-verbal communication – and I try to notice patterns. While I do this, I am mindful of being present, so I hold back from responding in any way. Of course I acknowledge what is being said, and then I ask myself a few questions, which may include:

'How can I impact this person, their business, or the community for the better?'

'Who else do I know who would benefit from sharing this connection?'

'How can I bring people together and bring them to the table as a better version of themselves?'

As you meet new people, take the opportunity to listen and understand who has crossed your path, and as you do, create three questions you can ask of yourself in order to leave those around you in a better place. Remember, you only have the opportunity to create a first impression once. This impact can be with the intent that you leave them in a better place than when you first met them, so how will you begin this process moving forward? What impact will you aim to achieve?

If everyone asked these questions, the world would no doubt be a better place. And while you can't change how everybody thinks, you can change yourself. When you start asking these questions of yourself, you'll create a positive ripple effect that will touch your broader community. You'll be an inspiration for others to live their lives in the same fashion.

So, to circle back around, my passion is to look at ways to lift the baseline of where people start in life and in business, across the globe; to leave a positive footprint that others can follow. I want to know that my words and actions have a beneficial impact on those around me.

When you adopt this approach to your personal and business life, amazing things can happen. Don't worry if this isn't your default mindset yet, what is important is that it resonates for you, because then you can take the steps to get to exactly where you want to be.

Remembering that change is always about ourselves, but we can always bring others on the journey with us by showing them how.

I encourage you to be a leader where change is embraced and seen as a norm; in a way we can consider 'what else?' My goal is to help you see change in its best light, so let me start by explaining what change really means.

ACTION CREATES CHANGE

The pleasing thing about change is that many organisations and leaders have embraced the need for change. However, I ask if you could consider what this means for you and your business. Have you embraced the value and impact that policies can bring about in matters such as change, transformation, diversity and mentorship, amongst other things?

Have these practices been given the attention and time they deserve, with people across all areas of the business? I know most leaders want to consider them and have them be part of a new vision for their workplace, yet often the rollout appears to be more driven to meet a deadline and be included in a current policy.

Like everything else we have worked through in this book, the greatest impact for change is achieved through 'showing' our people why we have adopted these practices, and having open discussion to outline the impact to everyone across the business.

Taking the opportunity to explore each of these practices will ensure people feel included. They will see the collaboration and the change the action will bring to the business as a whole.

Furthermore, it will allow people to hear a different voice, a different perspective and, at times, opposing views. This in itself teaches us patience and acceptance of differences. This way of engaging and the creation of a safe space, delivers psychological safety which people need both at work and in their personal lives. Importantly, they know that no matter what they see, feel or experience, it is acceptable to share their perspective.

By doing and showing how we can be different and accept change, we create a platform we want others to be a part of. It is in the *doing* that results change. The process of *doing* (as opposed to talking about what you want to achieve) will bring people on the journey with you.

The *doing* also affects the relationship we have with change within ourselves, as we become more aware of our own triggers and actions. As we embrace this, we begin to recognise our sub-conscious biases and, perhaps, our privileges. It is only in these realisations that we begin to truly embrace all we thought we knew, but we didn't.

It is in these transparent reflections and conversations that we can see the true impact of change and transformation within ourselves, our people and our business.

If we do all these beneficial things, we will see lasting changes. Don't rush the process, change is not a race. Take the opportunity to go through the motions reflecting on your beliefs and values and address what is unique and important to you and your people.

This way, your team will feel like those important business concepts actually matter. If you follow the small measured steps outlined in this book, your people will see your commitment and they will be clear about your intentions with every stage.

Likewise, a similar approach can be considered with mentorship.

We've all heard about 'career advisors' and the 'buddy' programs. Businesses introduce these because they know mentorship is important. However, often the desired results are not achieved, and this is likely to occur if the programs are not completed with the consistency to bring about positive change.

My perspective on mentorship is a little less traditional – I guess I go against the grain. I don't think of a mentor simply as someone who has done the work and can therefore explain how things have been done in the past.

I am mindful that we live and work in an ever-changing landscape, and because of this I am willing to listen and be guided by those who can bring to my awareness the things I don't know, but would benefit from knowing.

As a mentor and mentee myself, I continue to learn and seek out mentors who challenge and develop me, so at times, my mentors have been people who are half my age.

I'm sure this doesn't make sense to those who see mentorship in a traditional sense. After all, how can a twenty-something-year-old be my mentor? I understand that my skill set is different than those of younger generations, but it is because of this that I know I have *a lot* to learn from them. If I am to truly be a great leader, I need to consider what I need to know so I can help to develop leaders today that will shape a better tomorrow.

So, by being a mentee, I am developing myself, whilst heightening my awareness of the things I don't know. This type of reflection and relationship with myself has taught me a great deal about listening, understanding and accepting. It is through these lenses that I have discovered what I consider real mentorship to be. In saying this, I also liken it to a mentorship approach you might see in a family business. In family businesses, we often see younger generations sitting at the table with their parents (yes the boardroom), and while they may not sit at the table as equals, it is with the intent they will sit at the helm one day.

Family businesses understand that they'll have to pass the baton on at some point, so they focus on true mentorship and inclusivity, to ensure their children are ready.

Parents, whilst wanting to share knowledge of 'how to', are often aware that they need to evolve. They know they must keep looking forward and are prepared to think outside of the box. They don't want to have cookie-cutter vision as they can see they are living in an environment which is rapidly changing, so they reverse the role of mentorship in seeking guidance from their children so they can remain relevant and, perhaps, stay ahead of the game.

They want their children to stand on their own and truly lead in changing times. Rather, they allow them to express their creativity and introduce novel ideas to the business. While mentoring their children, parents learn a lot along the way.

In moving forward, perhaps you too can take the opportunity to review these practices, and consider how this approach may benefit you, your people and your organisation. Consider the impact this could make when it comes to acceptance of change, diversity, inclusion and the new practices you wish to embrace.

As evolving leaders it is up to us to disrupt the old way of being, so we can deliver stewardship that will bring about change, and develop our leaders of today and that of our future, to ensure we shape a better tomorrow.

I know that as you read this, you can see the value, understand the impact and, more importantly, recognise the changes which can be embraced. You may need to find ways to break the status quo and, at times, this may appear to be challenging, but I also know you are a leader who wants more for themselves and those around them – because you are reading this book. I know you are now prepared to find your voice and stand up to be heard. You are prepared to ask 'what else?'

There are so many steps we can take, and each one is slightly different depending on what you want to champion, but you now have some suggestions on how to look at things with a different lens. As you continue to surge forward, let me help you do it courageously.

CHANGE IS THE NEW NORM – OVERCOMING RESISTANCE TO CHANGE

We've all heard lots of messages about change, some of which have a negative framework around them, such as:

'Change is never easy.'
'You never know what the future holds.'

Although these sayings elicit an element of fear, we also know how important change is to deliver success. This is why we might see change as a necessary evil, but that does not need to be the case.

It's time for a new mindset which will help you recognise change for what it really is – a norm; part of everything around us. Let's see what you have to do to understand change in this light.

1. Help Your People See That Change Is a Normal Thing

I genuinely believe that change happens all the time. Whilst I see change in this light, I also know the power of consistency, so how can we bring the two together?

The way I look at it is; consistency applies to my values and the way I do things in life and at work. When I have solid foundations and clear boundaries, this all helps to create consistency in my communication and the way I engage. But when it comes to concrete action, events and everything in the outside world, I take every opportunity to introduce a change.

If you look around, you'll notice those same changes are happening to you on a daily basis. Some changes you purposefully initiate, while others come from external circumstances. Either way, change is constant and inevitable.

When you see it in this way, you can release most of the fear surrounding change. You'll notice it's already happening, no matter how you feel about it. So, you might as well choose to see change as the norm. This simple shift in mindset will create a different emotion within you when you now hear the word 'change'.

For me, change is putting one foot in front of the other. It's about progress, elevation and evolution. It's about stretching a little bit further and asking 'what else?' and 'who else?' and being open to new things, new people and a different voice. There's nothing scary or risky about it. When you see that you're accepting to listen to a different perspective, you are beginning the cycle a little differently. You are implementing changes across all areas of your life, a little at a time, and with these slight shifts you will diffuse the negativity you previously had attached to it.

It is at this point you can show others 'how'. You can show people the benefits that arise from change. Once you help others adopt this mind-set, you'll only ever move *forward*.

2. LISTEN FIRST, AND THEN UNDERSTAND

You can often feel when someone resists change. Some people will openly tell you this is the case. With that in mind, it's not about whether some-one resists change or not – it's about *why* they resist.

Everyone fears change for different reasons. Some people have had unpleasant experiences in the past, which leads to them being afraid now. Others are anxious about the inherent uncertainty that the future brings.

In any case, it is important to look at uncovering the reason why your people (or even yourself), fear change. To do this, you must listen.

I mentioned earlier the importance of active listening in Chapter III, and change resistance is another situation in which this skill is invaluable.

By listening to 'understand', you will soon discover the difference it holds over listening to 'respond'. I encourage you to reflect on this and ask you to equally listen for what people are not saying. We all need to be mindful of every conversation we have, and to create the space for people to breathe, think and then tell us what they can and want to share, in order to uncover the subtle things we can't hear outright.

The thing is, if we open our mind to more than just words, we'll see what sits behind the fear of change, and it is with this insight we can begin to bring about the changes we want to embrace.

3. Understand the Fear that Drives Resistance

In addition, it is important to try to pinpoint the exact fear that causes resistance to change. What is it that makes people feel a change may threaten them? For instance, an employee may feel the change will impact their job security. This is not an irrational fear considering how quickly we're moving towards automation and AI technologies, or even the recent impact on businesses throughout the pandemic. Many employees fear their jobs will become redundant, as businesses embrace new technologies or pivot to meet new demands.

Another common fear your employees may have is a lack of support. They might believe there will be no visible commitment or communication from leadership. As a result, your people may be afraid they won't have what they need to initiate change.

Of course, these are only a few of the many fears that result in resistance, so I encourage you to have open and honest communication that will leave no room for interpretation or horror stories in your people's minds. Let everyone voice their concerns, and don't judge their thoughts and emotions as you hear them.

Remember that fear is a powerful emotion, and you can't blame someone for feeling what they feel. Instead, you help them to overcome their fears through empathy and compassion. They need to see you will support them through their experiences.

4. Focus on Overcoming Resistance Before the Change Starts

During the change process, you could start executing a strategy immediately after planning it. By doing so, you may not leave enough time to address resistance. At times, it's not until the changes are well underway that you realise your team is hesitant.

This can cause tension and division and prevent you from initiating the change efficiently, or worse still, employees may get demotivated or give up altogether while you try to get everyone on board.

For this reason, it is important to address any resistance before you start to roll out the plan.

Including your people from the outset and keeping them engaged at every stage, is critical to ensure you are all aligned as you aim for success. Nipping resistance in the bud is essential, but it is also important that your people feel they have contributed to the process.

When people get involved in the planning stages, it allows you the opportunity to identify any concerns in a timely manner. Encourage your team to speak up; do it openly, so as one person shares their thoughts, others will see you genuinely want to hear what they have to say. When everyone's opinion is heard, you can clearly see how everyone feels about the proposed changes.

Once you've created the plan, set aside time to address any leftover resistance. Encourage everyone to speak about any fears or blocks that may prevent them from embracing the change. You can do this both as a collective and privately, especially if you identify anyone holding back.

This kind of proactivity will create a 'trust' environment and will undoubtedly make everything simpler as changes are introduced.

If you know your people are truly on board with the plan, you can confidently go about executing the strategy.

5. Leverage Your Leaders to Help Overcome Resistance

While face time with every employee is the best way to remove resistance, it's not possible in all situations. This is especially true in large organisations with hundreds, or even thousands, of people and even more challenging when you have teams across different states or even continents.

Luckily, you don't need to speak to everyone directly and in person, but it is important that you ensure everyone receives the same message and that the message is communicated with the same vision. To do this simply, select a few key people who share your commitment, and ask them to join you in delivering the message.

For instance, having your senior managers become excited about the change will ensure your cohesion is seen, which is extremely beneficial. They can advocate for you and the strategy being developed. They'll deliver positive words about the change and foster the right atmosphere around it.

I suggest you take this a step further and reach out to middle management and your supervisors as well. They're often closer to your employees than your senior staff, so they will bridge any potential communication gaps, and your message can be heard by all involved.

Using this approach will allow you to address any concerns they may have, so they too can communicate clearly with their teams. It is important they don't feel any resistance, as this can easily spill onto the teams they manage. To create alignment, you must make sure every manager is on the same page when it comes to your strategy.

Of course, you can expect lots of feedback, so make sure to listen and embrace suggestions with openness and ease. Encourage your managers to highlight anyone with struggles or concerns, so that you can help them out too.

6. BE EXCITED ABOUT THE CHANGE YOU WANT TO CREATE

As we have previously identified, communication about the changes alone are not enough. It is incredibly important to communicate the reasons behind any change, as this gives your people the opportunity to understand the motivation, as well as share in the vision, and subsequently, stay focused.

By being genuine and sharing your excitement for the change, your people will be able to relate to you. Be open and show them you are both excited, and even nervous, or whatever emotion you are experiencing.

It's important to be authentic and transparent. I always try to imagine the outcome the change will create, and how it will benefit everyone involved. This helps to alleviate any fear and creates a positive energy, showing everyone you are excited about what the future holds.

Energy is contagious, so make sure to spread the right kind across your organisation.

Of course, it's vital to maintain the excitement as you go about executing the change strategy. It creates the consistency I talked about earlier, so you already know how important it is. Keeping energy levels high throughout the process will minimise any resistance along the way.

CHANGE REQUIRES ACTION

I hope you can now see change in a more positive and healthier light. It's happening to us on some level every day, so there really is nothing to fear.

In fact, there's a positive change happening at this very moment. 2020 was a year of great change. How we have embraced it will be reflected in our perception of it. I see 2021 with a lens that shows we have all achieved a great deal in what we have learnt about ourselves and those around us. It is in this light that I look at this year as 2020 **WON.**

As you're reading this book, I know you are winning. You're learning how to raise the baseline for you and those around you, as you step into a new era of leadership. You're seeing what it takes to have a more positive impact on those around you, and how to generate better results as a consequence.

When the time comes to apply all that knowledge and skill, embrace the opportunity with both hands. Know that the future will be bright as long as you remain consistent and don't give up on change.

There are no guarantees in life, and nobody can predict the future, but change is up to you and there's something that will help get you closer … I'll tell you about it in the next chapter.

Top Takeaways

1. If we open our mind to more than just words, we'll see what sits behind the fear of change, and it is with this insight we can begin to bring about the changes we want to embrace.

2. Fear is a powerful emotion, and you can't blame someone for feeling what they feel. Instead, you help them to overcome their fears through empathy and compassion.

3. Encourage your managers to highlight anyone with struggles or concerns, so that you can help them out too.

4. Energy is contagious, so make sure to spread the right kind across your organisation.

5. When the time comes to apply all that knowledge and skill, embrace the opportunity with both hands.

VII

Are You a Leader Who Can Communicate the Ending at the Beginning?

Have you heard about starting with the end in mind? It's a relatively new concept compared to the way we've traditionally done business. As such, it's not as accepted as I believe it should be.

I see many big corporations adapting agile leadership, which is great, as they operate under the assumption that the future will involve change. The 'agile' values and principles encourage leaders to use collaboration and to empower others to grow and share in the decision-making. Amongst other things, they look at failures as opportunities to learn.

In theory, this concept is solid. As circumstances around you change, you change your direction as well. By doing so, you get to adapt, evolve, and eventually, succeed.

So here is an added step which will enable you and your team to succeed. It starts at the beginning. When you are rolling out your project, it would be of great benefit to invest time, up front, to *really* consider what the desired outcome needs to be. Stop and think about who the changes are for, what the desired outcome is, and whether you are considering the changes through your lens or the intended recipient. When organisations consider enhancements and changes, they often look to be the best in the market or better than their competitor. Although this may be valid, does that mean their benchmark is what *clients* are actually asking for?

Does it mean the potential issues, wants and needs of the clients will be achieved? Achieving the desired outcome is not always what we believe is needed, it's more about what is wanted and required by the client. Adding this step may better equip us to reach the desired outcome.

If you recall the phrase that I have shared with you, that my client shared with me, one that I always keep in mind as I begin a new engagement – 'I didn't know what I didn't know.' Taking the time to actually 'be the client' and identify things which make their experience better, faster and easier, is where we need to start.

Bringing everyone in at the beginning and sharing the key objectives, so they can all contribute to being part of the solution before a project is planned and rolled out, will bring about the changes you desire.

More so, your team can seek out the support of others in the team, and this brings more people on the journey who are part of the solution from the onset.

Would you like to bring some predictability for the future, and provide your people with more confidence?

Well, you can!

Being a leader who communicates the ending from the outset, allows you to reverse-engineer the steps to get exactly where you need to be. This creates more certainty and brings confidence to the plan you and your team put into motion.

Let's start with a necessary prerequisite.

WHAT ELSE DOES A LEADER DO THAT CAN COMMUNICATE THE ENDING AT THE BEGINNING?

Of course, it starts with the end in mind, but this alone isn't enough to create the future you've envisioned. There are a few boxes that you must tick to execute a successful plan.

And it all starts with you stepping back a little.

You see, many leaders are eager to push forward when making plans for the future. Often, they believe they already have the solution, and with this in mind, they assume everyone is on board and will 'fall into line' with their vision and strategy.

However, this kind of thinking can be detrimental. We can't possibly understand the ramifications of every action our teams will take within a strategy. More importantly, we don't have to. All we need to do is stick to the things we're already good at, and for everything else, find the right people to sit at the boardroom table with us.

No matter how capable we are, we have weaknesses. Luckily, there are others who compliment us. Leveraging people is a fantastic way to take a holistic approach to being a great leader.

When we start with the end in mind, we can focus too much on the outcome we want to create. As a result, we may fail to address opportunities and/or threats. That's when having the right people by our side is immensely valuable. They can help us identify any opportunities we may have missed and remedy them before we even begin.

Once we have our trusted team, it's time to start working backwards from our goal. And if you need proof of how valuable this can be, there's a plethora of information out there.

For instance, research published in *Psychological Science* examined the effect that goal-planning methods have on the end result. Five studies encompassed students and their approach to coursework, comprehensive exams and important job interviews.

One group planned all their activities in the usual, chronological order. The other group visualised their goals and worked their way backwards.

Now, for simple and short-term goals, there wasn't much difference in these methods, but for larger goals which required time and effort, the difference was more than obvious. The group who planned in reverse had a much higher success rate than their counterparts.

Why?

Because the first group suffered from classic issues related to chronological planning – feelings of distance from their goal, idea rumination, related anxiety and others.

At the same time, the group who started with the end in mind, felt much more confident and motivated during their work. The reason for this is the fundamental benefit of planning backwards.

When you plan in reverse, you operate under the assumption that all your steps already worked. You're not second-guessing or hoping you'll get it right, and as a result you get an increase in confidence.

So, how can you reap these benefits in full? Let's see how you can embrace the skill of leading with the end in mind.

GETTING REVERSE PLANNING RIGHT – THE KEY STEPS

If you've been planning chronologically, it may take a little to adjust to the idea of reverse planning. Fortunately, the concept is straightforward enough.

Here are the tangible steps you can take:

1. Start with Your Goal

Of course, this is the first and most important step that you must get right. You can't draw the right road map if you don't know the exact destination.

Because of this, you must be as specific with your goal as possible. Find a way to quantify it and create a precise desired outcome. Once you do, bring different people within your team together so you can share your vision with them.

This will be a great opportunity for you to establish if you are clear in your message and your vision. Their feedback and insight will also allow you the opportunity to consider 'what else?'

Ask yourself if the goal is achievable. While you should always be ambitious, setting unrealistic goals will result in wasted time and frustration. It is important to ensure you are not setting anyone up to fail and you are able to deliver the outsome so everyone can succeed. The objective is to find the sweet spot and set a crystal-clear goal you can all work towards.

2. Identify the Steps Needed to Reach That Goal

Working backwards from your goal, set out to identify the steps you need to achieve. Imagine yourself achieving the goal and think of the step right before that happens. Then follow the same pattern, identify the steps needed prior to that, so you can create a sequence. Don't rush this process and ensure you include your team as you make each decision.

Now, this may take quite some time and effort. It also pays to have a high-performing leadership team, each of them may identify steps and circumstances you could miss on your own.

It's a good idea to group all the steps you need to take into clusters.

Doing so makes it easier to visualise and structure a plan. Instead of getting overwhelmed by all those steps, you'll get a bird's-eye view of the whole process. So take your time and plan each step carefully, then move on to the next step. Look at any interdependencies and ensure you have all parties involved with full collaboration.

3. Attach Deadlines and Milestones to Those Steps

No matter how big or small, all goals must be time bound. There's little point in planning if you don't know whether you're meeting the necessary deadlines.

Because of this, add those deadlines to each step as you define them. Again, you should start with the end goal and determine when you want to achieve it. Like the goal itself, the date should be specific and realistic.

As you assign dates to each of the steps, you may notice some deviations to the original end date. This isn't an issue, and you definitely shouldn't cut any process short for the purpose of strictly meeting the end date.

What you should do is allow some breathing room. The reason you'll start with the end date isn't to predict the future, it's to ensure you are not over-allocating too much time for each of the steps. As you try to squeeze them all into the defined time frame, you'll ensure efficiency. And if you end up having to postpone the end date, you'll know it's for a good reason.

4. Remember This Is a Process (So Don't Rush It)

Related to the above step, the last thing you want to do is rush the planning process. There will be many moving parts to figure out and fixing them in the right place can require some time and planning.

Even though this way of planning differs from the traditional, it still follows the fundamental rule:

'A good plan is half the job done.'

If your plan isn't solid, your execution won't be either. Remember the whole purpose of reverse planning is to have a clear outline of everything you need to do to reach the desired outcome. There are no shortcuts, you don't want to miss any important considerations.

5. ENGAGE YOUR TEAM TO CREATE AN EFFECTIVE PLAN

Once you have all the measured steps outlined with their corresponding dates (yes, setting a date is a critical part of the process), let your team help you create an effective plan. Each member of your team needs to feel the plan is realistic, which is why you need to engage with them throughout the process. Take on board any feedback they provide. Your listening to understand is vital here, as they will be the ones communicating the changes with their team on the frontline.

As discussed in the previous chapter, this process will help you combat any resistance. It also ensures alignment across the entire business; everyone will know their part and how much time they have to do the necessary work.

This is how you get all your people on the same page, figuratively and literally. So, involve your people from the beginning, and allow them time to create solutions and identify ways they can contribute. More importantly this will create alignment and collaboration amongst the team, as well as increase productivity and positive energy.

Top Takeaways

1. Being a leader who communicates the ending from the outset allows you to reverse-engineer the steps to get exactly where you need to be.

2. When you plan in reverse, you operate under the assumption that all your steps already worked. You're not second-guessing or hoping you'll get it right, and as a result you get an increase in confidence.

3. 5-step plan-in-reverse tips: start with your goal, identify the steps needed to reach that goal, attach deadlines and milestones to those steps, remember this is a process (so don't rush it) and engage your team to create an effective plan.

VIII

BEING A POSITIVE INFLUENCE

I know being someone of influence is not always something you think about when you think about leadership, however, it is with this skill that we can create impact. As leaders, people naturally look to us for guidance and support, but what they really want from us is reassurance. They look to us to tell them things will work out and that their contributions have meaning.

While you take a moment to look at what you've done in the past to recognise this and what has worked, it is important to stand to the side a little and sit in a slightly different space.

Reflect on what has happened in those moments when you truly connected with your team. Knowing what you now know today, can you see the power you hold to influence, reassure and create an energy that will have a ripple effect and bring about a celebration for change? One where you can also provide a space for psychological safety?

THE CURATOR IN YOU

Many people believe it will take years of training, and that you must be gifted or have 'something special' to influence people. Others believe you need a title, hold a degree or doctorate, or perhaps come from a certain bloodline or wealthy family – but none of that really matters.

Truth be told, choosing to invest in any qualification will be helpful, however it's not something you can hang your hat on to get you to where you want to be. It is not what will make you influential, and certainly not the thing that will help you to lead with influence.

With so many talented people around the world, and those who are born into privileged and influential families, it is not their talent or birthright that will make them someone of influence. Influence is earned; it is brought about through respect and a commitment to do right by others.

Influence comes from you and your commitment to serve. People see the way you behave and the way in which you engage; your drive to bring about a better world and a better human race. It is these actions, beliefs and values which make you a person with influence.

A leader with influence, is someone who is prepared to stand with their people, who will walk alongside them, guide them, and is prepared to be their voice. This is you, the whole of you; the curator who aims to lift those around you.

1. START WITH HOW YOU SEE YOURSELF

Most of us have been told a story, whether it be in our personal or our professional life, and it is here I want you to start, because it is often a story we have heard so many times that it has now become a belief.

Looking inward allows us to reflect and consider what beliefs we have about ourselves. Being able to identify these beliefs will help us be more purposeful about the choices we make to bring about change. This reflective process takes time, and with every action something new will come up. Being aware, and making conscious decisions as you move forward, is where the magic is.

As a leader in our chosen profession, most of us look at our work and believe we have an obligation to fulfil, so we focus on the task at hand. After all, most businesses look at targets, statistics and key performance indicators, so we fall into line and identify with what we need to achieve and simply 'get on with it'. However, we don't stop to consider how we are seen and what influence we have on others.

It is how we approach our obligations, tasks and goals, together with the way we communicate with our people, that leads to building relationships, respect and trust. Our actions and the congruency which exists between what we say and what we do, will allow people to formulate their opinion of who we are and how we fit into their understanding of leadership. If we build trust and show people we value them, they will see us as a leader; trust starts a relationship where we can begin to influence. In the process, they will form an alignment with us and want to contribute and collaborate with us.

So, knowing what you know now, how will you continue to step forward, as you curate the leader within you, and be a positive influence?

2. RECOGNISING THE EASE

You know you are in the right place when you are enjoying what you do and find it 'easy'. Statistics have shown us we tend to be good with the things we love doing, so playing to your strengths will help you continue to be a positive influence.

The way we approach our work will enable us to shine and it is in these moments that people look to us and identify what they want for themselves. If we recognise these moments, we have an opportunity to use our influence to serve those around us.

Our purpose is to support others to find their place of ease; the place where they too may perform at their best and be happy to grow. As these moments arise, it is important to allow what comes naturally to you to be effective for others. It is here you can support and lift others so they too can shine.

Using your position of service, to step up and enable others to be seen with your support, creates influence. Using your voice for others, especially if they are yet to find their voice, is the key most important thing you can do, no matter how loud or to whom, that action alone begins their journey and their belief in themselves.

As soon as you have found your voice, using it becomes easy, so ensure to use it for others, which in turn will show them how they can use their voice too.

3. RIPPLE EFFECTS – THE POSITIVE IMPACT

We have all seen situations when people with influence can create a negative impact, so it is important to be aware of what you put into the universe. I know with you reading this book, that is not who you are, but it is important to be aware of how we engage and what influence we have on others.

Our influence creates an impact, not only through our words, but also in our actions and no matter what and how these may appear to others, it is up to us to ensure there is no room for misinterpretation, so being cohesive with our words and our actions is important.

I share the following example with you to bring to your awareness the importance of perception and how we can ensure what we intend is received with the right message, so it can create a positive ripple effect.

I am using the simple example of casting a stone into the lake. We can all see the stone as it hits the water create a motion, but what we take away may be different.

Some of us may see the action as a way to bring the motion and energy we have (a positive one that sees beauty in the circles being formed), expand and include others, so they too know how they can be fulfilled by the beauty which surrounds them. However, there may be others who see the stone as breaking a calm body of water, causing disruption and, as such, this action is now creating a negative impact.

So, in this case, your message that comes with the action of casting a stone is integral to how people receive what you have done.

When you have the opportunity to influence, be sure to also communicate your message with your action. Lead people in a way that will serve them to be the best version of themselves, and ensure it will lead them to place of fulfillment.

4. CREATING VALUE

As a leader your focus is to remain on adding value. It is important you continue to look at ways to contribute, whether it is to your people or to the business, and it is in these acts that people will recognise you as someone of influence. The act of lifting others as opposed to self, heightens people's awareness of who you are, what you do and how you do it but, more importantly, where your values lie.

In your drive to deliver value, it is important you also develop the ability to see anyone new, either in your wider circle or at work, as a potential new partner. Often in these situations, we see the new person as a potential competitor, but if you shift your mindset at the onset and consider that they may be there to support and bring added value, their introduction could be viewed as someone who can help you redefine your unique contribution, as well as contribute to adding value to those around you.

DIMARCHOS

With this outlook, competitors will never make you fear your own position, in fact, they will enable you to redefine your drive to create positive impact, and invigorate you, as you continue to evolve and contribute at a higher level.

While others in these moments stay close to monitor the new person so they can see what they do and who they are, you can take the opportunity to step back and allow them to step up and shine. You will act with encouragement and in doing so, this will break old patterns and behaviours, showing others that new ways of driving collaboration can not only add value to the business, but create psychological safety for everyone involved.

When we create a safe place for a new person, we also re-enforce safety for our existing staff. This embraced behaviour naturally stimulates creativity, mindfulness and acceptance.

5. Being Seen

While we can now acknowledge that we are seen as someone of influence, it is important we show people that they too can do what we do. Sharing your experiences, be it easy, hard, fun or even challenging, demystifies any perception that exists in what it takes to be a leader and someone of influence.

It is important to know it does not diminish your position in any way, but instead strengthens it, as they see you are genuine and transparent in wanting them to rise and be the best version of themselves.

The new version of leadership is not about withholding knowledge; it is to share everything you know so everyone around you rises. This is how we begin to raise the baseline across the globe.

Your ability to be honest and transparent allows people to see that they can do it too. The more people of influence we have across the globe, the greater impact we can create, as we collaborate to serve others. This then ensures that our movement to lift the baseline from where people start in life will be magnified.

Being seen in the world is about creating a path so others can follow. Showing them how, and then allowing them to do it in their unique way, ensures they stay true to themselves.

6. MOBILITY – IS IT AN ASSET OR A HINDRANCE TO INFLUENCE?

In my journey of listening, I have heard our future generation share some of their thoughts, and it is with this lens I share my vision and belief that by 2040, we will see most millennials move to the entrepreneurship model of employment. The driving factor behind this is so they can continue to expand their knowledge base, while also assuring themselves they can maintain a lifestyle that serves them best.

Historically, people have held onto a traditional model of having a career (me included, until recently), one where we held roles for perhaps 10, 15 or more years. But the business world is moving rapidly, so planning for what is needed in the future will see roles, positions and careers redefined.

Right now, your most valuable asset as an individual is your ability and willingness to grow and develop, but it is also about your reach. The number of people who know you, like you and trust you, will have an impact, along with your unique outlook. Your ability to look at anything with a different lens for the way forward, will define who you are and how you are seen.

Every exposure and experience you have and your ability to review and accept differences, will develop and expand your knowledge base. Moving in circles that will enable you to consider 'what else?' will help you to overcome obstacles and bring you closer to being a person who can influence others with your uniqueness.

Your uniqueness is what people will remember.

Every business opportunity you are exposed to will drive the stories you share – they form your experiences (not just with work, but your engagement with people).

It is important though, that with every engagement, you continue to focus on adding value, as well as lifting and contributing to those around you. So, as you continue on your journey to lead, know that your trail, your footprint and your actions will create an impact and no matter where you are and where you are going, others will follow.

The road is yours to create, and the greater your experiences, the more you will be able to add value to those around you. You will bring about change and create greater influence through experience.

Top Takeaways

1. Being conscious and congruent in our language and our actions will create trust, which is the basis of every relationship.

2. Your ability to influence will create a ripple effect, so be sure you know what impact you want to create.

3. Ripple effects – the positive impact.

4. Stepping up, being seen, and having a voice gives others permission to do the same, so don't hold back. Stand up and be you.

IX

It's a Muscle That Needs to Be Activated, Stretched, but Most of All, Used Daily

Well, where do I start? I guess it has to be to share this one, very valuable, thing with you; I don't have it all. I don't know it all and, as you can see, despite where I have been and the work I do, I continue to learn and be guided. Through each of these strategies, I look for opportunities to lift up, give back or pay it forward.

So I guess I have to start by giving gratitude to all the amazing humans who have crossed my path, and to those whom I will have the fortunate pleasure of meeting in years to come.

There are so many people who have contributed to me being who I am today. By being on this journey with you, I have learnt a great deal about myself from my teams; the people with heart and soul, courage, faith and commitment to have achieved what we did as a collective. I am also grateful to my clients, who trust in me their journey, where we shift and embrace the changes they and their teams are about to embark on. And of course, thank you to the leaders of tomorrow, you who are reading this book, in having the commitment to work towards lifting the baseline of others.

The most important thing I take away through all of these experiences and lessons in leadership, is a commitment from me to 'life learning'. Using this muscle each day, so I can continue to serve and learn, will ensure that my voice is used for the good of others, and they too will do the same for someone else.

1. IT IS NOT A DESTINATION

Leadership is not found at any one destination, nor is it something that is reached when in a particular position. It is not a title or an accolade; it is something we need to continue to monitor, reflect, act upon and grow with.

Leadership is a muscle that, if not worked on, will weaken and perhaps disappear, or even cause a negative impact. It is something which requires input, feedback, reflection and a commitment to do more and be more.

We alone do not have the ability or the capacity to teach ourselves how to lead better, we need interaction. What we need to support us in our commitment of service, is to continually seek input from those around us. It is important in this process that we seek out feedback from a cross-section of people and ensure we are not simply receiving feedback people think we want to hear, but genuine feedback so we may continue to grow.

Our journey of leadership, whilst we are there or when we are striving toward it, should be seen through the lens of who is on the journey with us – 'Who else will benefit from coming along and where do I need to take them?' Leadership should be visible and in displaying it to the world, we can show others the highs, the troughs and everything in-between. It needs to be seen for what it is, with all its imperfections. In saying this, don't wait to have things perfect before stepping up, as this will make it difficult for others to follow.

2. WABI-SABI – CELEBRATING UNIQUENESS

Historically, we have identified people in key positions as our leaders, but today we identify leadership with so much more. As mentioned earlier, it is not about titles, anyone can step up to lead at any age and with any purpose.

Our global economy continues to change and leadership is now based more on potential and innovation. With this in mind, leadership lends itself to being more about people who choose to dedicate their time for the improvement of others, and to those who are committed to dedicating their time, money and anything else to the improvement of humanity and our planet.

The leaders of today are extraordinary people who have not mastered the art of leading, but are prepared to stand up, even if they are standing alone. They are prepared to be seen as the individual they are – with all their imperfections. It is this skill which is most admired by us all.

Not feeling they need to be perfect and more importantly not feeling that they need to know everything, leaders of today show the world their passion and purpose. To serve for the good of humanity instantly places them in a position of leadership, indeed one of influence.

The Japanese philosophy of wabi-sabi celebrates beauty in what is natural – flaws and all. I believe this is what our future generation needs to see in our leaders, because it is real, it is achievable and it celebrates every individual for being exactly who they are, not who others want them to be.

The appreciation of honesty, rawness and humility that is shown by our leaders of tomorrow, is what most people today find appealing and is what creates a following – they are our influencers of tomorrow.

3. CONTENT, RECIPES AND DETAILS

I shared earlier with you the power that knowledge holds, but more specifically that it only holds power when shared. As this point, I would like to suggest, as a deliberate act each day, if you use your knowledge daily and share it, you will continue evolving.

Your thoughts, your vision and your story when shared, will contribute to the rising of others. When we can share not just the end result, but the thought process and the reasons why we make certain decisions, others around us may begin to understand our line of thinking. It is like teaching people to fish, instead of just bringing the food to them.

The processes and thought patterns we consider as we prepare a strategy or a plan are equally important to that of the end goal when we share knowledge. It is like sharing the ingredients in a recipe; we must give the measurements as well as sharing the preparation details, so others have the ability to not only bake, but to ensure it will taste brilliant too.

The gifting of knowledge in this way is invaluable as it shows others exactly how you have made your food, and allows them to also be creative and make adjustments if they want to create their own version of the recipe, which then becomes authentic to them.

This level of detail and support is similar to that which I share when I walk my clients through the 'small measured steps' in *The Fundamentals of Business,* when they are either starting up or scaling a business. Sometimes they know where they want to be, but setting up each step and following it through to reach success can get lost in the planning, if not outlined in detail and set up properly at the outset.

Every time you go through the process, you adapt and learn, and this expands your unique proposition too – it helps you to strengthen your muscle.

4. Strength in Anti-Fragility

Building resilience and supporting one another in the past year has been a focal point, however this journey has not ended. The way in which we have connected is not a one-time event, it has changed who we are and what we want, not only for ourselves, but that of others too.

In the process, we have been challenged personally, but in our continual pursuit to serve others, we have been able to grow ourselves. We have gained insight through experience as opposed to reading or hearing about it. More importantly, we have as a whole, become more understanding and more accepting of differences.

We have become more aware and more patient. We have encouraged our people to work with tools which help them move forward, and allow them the freedom to have a voice, expressing their thoughts. This is what is needed to help all of us on the road to recovery.

Self-awareness has been a muscle well exercised, and our emotional intelligence has been heightened, allowing us to engage more effectively.

So with this as a reflection, we can keep looking forward at what else we can do to support everyone around us. What other tools, skills and muscles can we put into place to help us build leaders today so that we have a better tomorrow?

With resilience being at the top of the list, I would like to suggest we add 'grit' to our toolkits. Developing 'grit' together with resilience will potentially help develop a somewhat different tool – 'anti-fragility.'

The term 'anti-fragility' was conceived by Nassim Nicholas Taleb; a mathematical statistician and former option trader and risk analyst, whose work concerns problems of randomness, probability and uncertainty.

According to Taleb, when we develop anti-fragility, we are able to create an environment where we increase our capability to thrive as a result of stressors. The difference being that with resilience we resist challenges, but with anti-fragility, we get better.

*'Some things benefit from shocks; they thrive and grow when exposed to volatility, randomness, disorder and stressors, and love, adventure, risk and uncertainty. Yet, in spite of the ubiquity of the phenomenon, there is no word for the exact opposite of fragile. Let us call it anti-fragile. Anti-fragility is beyond resilience or robustness. The resilient resists shocks and stays the same; the **anti-fragile gets better.'***

'In essence it follows the same concept as "what doesn't break you makes you stronger".' – Nassim Nicholas Taleb

So how can we help ourselves and our teams to become anti-fragile, to keep surging forward having learnt from our experiences, especially our most challenging ones?

1. Create very simple rules
2. Be connected to what you are doing (purpose-driven)
3. Build in backups (I call it shadowing – so that you don't set anyone or anything up as a single point to potentially fail)
4. Minimise risks that have absolutes (if something fails – it's okay, not catastrophic)
5. Consider 'what else?' and experiment with small risks

If at this very moment you are thinking that you want to explore more, great – because that is what great leadership is about; opening up to differences and allowing the conversation to take place, to take a step back and look at what you have accomplished. Acknowledge your commitment and passion to serve and accept that others will want to do the same for you too.

ARE YOU READY TO LEAD?

We often talk about how the business landscape keeps changing rapidly, but some of the changes we make are slow and, to be honest, perhaps done so in a way where we are playing it safe.

This is your opportunity to change things! Do you share my vision for the future, where organisations thrive based on openness, alignment, consistency and a purpose to serve others? Do you believe each leader has the ability and power to bring profound transformation on a global scale? If so, you now understand what it takes to step into this new world of leadership.

As you have seen throughout this book, there are some key differences we can embrace to bring about the change we want to see in the world.

So, as you step forward, think limitlessly and embrace your full potential so you can create a prosperous future for those around you.

Cast that stone, share your story and watch the ripple effect envelop those around you to bring joy, creativity and strength so we can create a better tomorrow.

Take what you've learned in this book together with your unique knowledge, step up and make it happen! I believe in you and your commitment to lift and serve others.

And if you need more help, feel free to reach out to me at:
info@solutions2you.com.au

Let's make the business world a better place – one where we have people at the centre of everything we do!

Top Takeaways

1. The most important thing I take away, through all of these experiences and lessons in leadership, is a commitment from me to 'life learning'.

2. Leadership is not found at any one destination, it is something we need to continue to monitor, reflect, act upon and grow with.

3. Our global economy continues to change and leadership is now based more on potential and innovation.

4. Your thoughts, your vision and your story when shared, will contribute to the rising of others.

5. Self-awareness has been a muscle well exercised, and our emotional intelligence has been heightened, allowing us to engage more effectively.

6. When we develop anti-fragility, we are able to create an environment where we increase our capability to thrive as a result of stressors.

Printed in Australia
AUHW020401230522
363979AU00003B/6

9 780645 166903